Debbie Mumm's Cozy Northwest Christmas

Create a colorful and cozy Christmas with this heartwarming collection of quilts and projects inspired by the friendly animals to a forest of pine trees, from snuggly snowmen, you'll find a season full of qu

DEBBIE MUMM

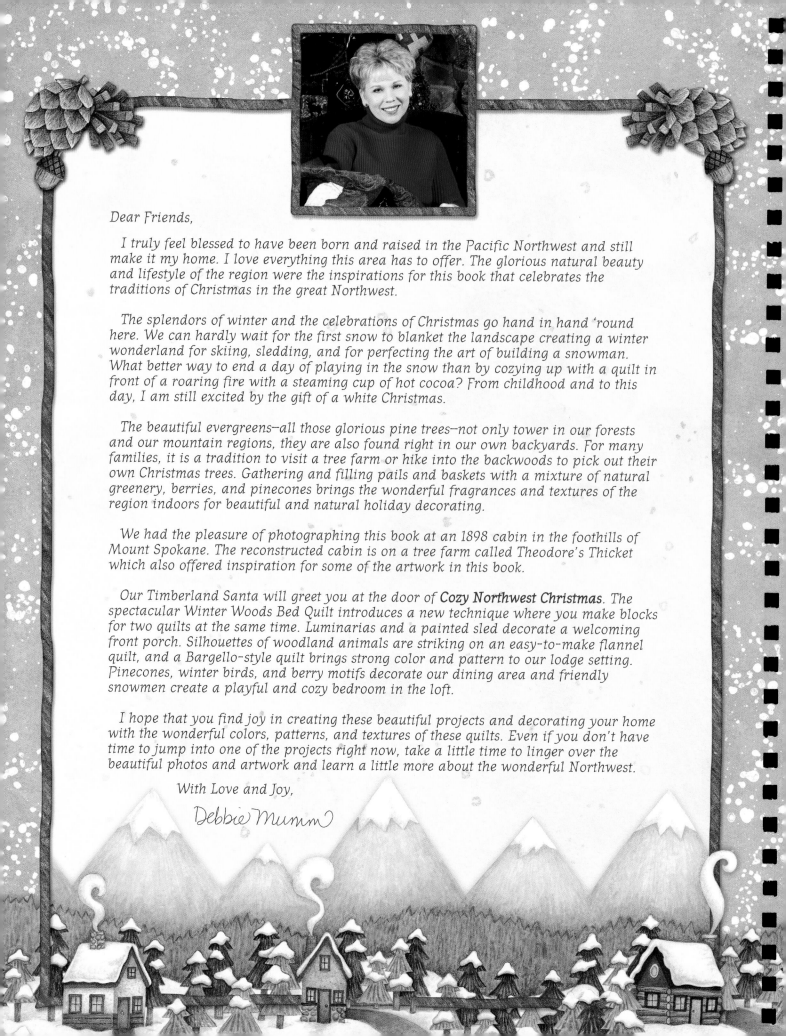

Dear Friends,

I truly feel blessed to have been born and raised in the Pacific Northwest and still make it my home. I love everything this area has to offer. The glorious natural beauty and lifestyle of the region were the inspirations for this book that celebrates the traditions of Christmas in the great Northwest.

The splendors of winter and the celebrations of Christmas go hand in hand 'round here. We can hardly wait for the first snow to blanket the landscape creating a winter wonderland for skiing, sledding, and for perfecting the art of building a snowman. What better way to end a day of playing in the snow than by cozying up with a quilt in front of a roaring fire with a steaming cup of hot cocoa? From childhood and to this day, I am still excited by the gift of a white Christmas.

The beautiful evergreens—all those glorious pine trees—not only tower in our forests and our mountain regions, they are also found right in our own backyards. For many families, it is a tradition to visit a tree farm or hike into the backwoods to pick out their own Christmas trees. Gathering and filling pails and baskets with a mixture of natural greenery, berries, and pinecones brings the wonderful fragrances and textures of the region indoors for beautiful and natural holiday decorating.

We had the pleasure of photographing this book at an 1898 cabin in the foothills of Mount Spokane. The reconstructed cabin is on a tree farm called Theodore's Thicket which also offered inspiration for some of the artwork in this book.

Our Timberland Santa will greet you at the door of **Cozy Northwest Christmas**. The spectacular Winter Woods Bed Quilt introduces a new technique where you make blocks for two quilts at the same time. Luminarias and a painted sled decorate a welcoming front porch. Silhouettes of woodland animals are striking on an easy-to-make flannel quilt, and a Bargello-style quilt brings strong color and pattern to our lodge setting. Pinecones, winter birds, and berry motifs decorate our dining area and friendly snowmen create a playful and cozy bedroom in the loft.

I hope that you find joy in creating these beautiful projects and decorating your home with the wonderful colors, patterns, and textures of these quilts. Even if you don't have time to jump into one of the projects right now, take a little time to linger over the beautiful photos and artwork and learn a little more about the wonderful Northwest.

With Love and Joy,

Debbie Mumm

Table of Contents

Soft lights twinkle
through lustrous luminarias
lighting the way for arriving
guests. A sled and ice skates
are ready by the cabin door.
A cozy quilt waits on the
rocker to add warmth to the
late afternoon sunlight.
And Santa stands ready
to welcome family
and friends home.

Northwest
Welcome

Timberland Santa
Door Banner

Finished size:
29" x 49"

What does Santa do during the off-season?
I believe he lives in a cabin in the Pacific Northwest surrounded by forest-creature friends!
Wherever you live, our Timberland Santa will be right at home
providing a warm welcome message on your front door.

Fabric Requirements and Cutting Instructions

Read all instructions before beginning and use ¼"-wide seam allowances throughout. Read Cutting Strips and Pieces on page 108 prior to cutting fabrics.

Timberland Santa Door Banner 29" x 49"	FIRST CUT		SECOND CUT	
	Number of Strips or Pieces	Dimensions	Number of Pieces	Dimensions
Fabric A Background ½ yard	1	5" x 42"	2	5" x 11½"
	1	4½" x 42"	2	4½" x 10½"
			2	3½" x 5½"
			2	3½" squares
	2	2½" x 42"	2	2½" x 21½"
			2	2½" squares
	1	1½" x 42"	1	1½" x 8½"
			2	1½" x 3½"
			4	1½" squares
			2	1" squares
Fabric B* Coat ⅓ yard	1	5½" x 42"	1	5½" x 14½"
			2	5" x 3"
			2	4" x 3½"
	1	3½" x 42"	2	3½" x 4½"
			2	2½" squares
			1	1" x 11½"
Fabrics C–M on adjacent chart.				

BORDERS

	FIRST CUT		SECOND CUT	
Fabric N Sawtooth Border and Triangles ⅞ yard	1	5" x 42"	2	5" squares
	8	2½" x 42"	2	2½" x 40½"
			2	2½" x 20½"
			60	2½" squares
Fabric O Sawtooth Border Triangles ½ yard	1	5" x 42"	2	5" squares
	4	2½" x 42"	60	2½" squares
Binding ⅜ yard	4	2¾" x 42"		

Moustache and Eyebrow Appliqués - Scraps
Mitten Appliqués - ⅙ yard
Backing - 1½ yards
Batting - 33" x 53"
Fusible Web (optional)
1" Pom-pom
Embroidery Floss or Perle Cotton
Buttons: Two 1" and two ⅜"

For directional fabric, the size that is listed first runs parallel to selvage (strip width). You may wish to "fussy cut" pieces to match plaid. See page 108.

Timberland Santa Door Banner Continued	FIRST CUT	
	Number of Strips or Pieces	Dimensions
Fabric C Pants ⅓ yard	1	8½" x 11½"
Fabric D Boots ⅛ yard	1	3" x 18½"
	1	1½" x 11½"
Fabric E Boot Sole Scrap	3	1" x 6½"
Fabric F Socks Scrap	1	2½" x 11½"
Fabric G Top Log* ⅜ yard	1	12" x 8"
Fabric H Bottom Log Scrap	1	11½" x 4½"
Fabric I Beard ⅙ yard	1	5" x 8½"
	2	2" x 4"
Fabric J Face Scrap	1	4" x 5½"
Fabric K Hat Scrap	1	2½" x 8½"
Fabric L Hat Accent Scrap	1	1½" x 8½"
Fabric M Hat Top and Mitten Trim Appliqué ⅛ yard	1	1½" x 8½"
Fabrics N–O on adjacent chart.		

Making the Quilt

The Timberland Santa Door Banner is constructed using quick corner triangles, half-square triangles, quick-fuse appliqué, and embroidery. Refer to Accurate Seam Allowance on page 108 prior to making project.

Assembling the Center Panel

1. Sew 1½" x 8½" Fabric L piece between 1½" x 8½" Fabric M piece and 2½" x 8½" Fabric K piece as shown. Press.

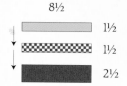

2. Refer to Quick Corner Triangles on page 108. Sew two 2½" Fabric A squares to unit from step 1 as shown. Press.

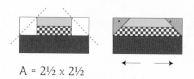

A = 2½ x 2½

3. Making quick corner triangle units, sew two 2½" Fabric B squares to 5" x 8½" Fabric I piece as shown. Press.

B = 2½ x 2½
I = 5 x 8½

4. Sew 4" x 5½" Fabric J piece between two 2" x 4" Fabric I pieces as shown. Press. Sew this unit to unit from step 3 as shown. Press.

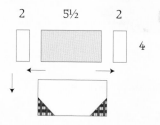

5. Making quick corner triangle units, sew 3½" Fabric A square to 3½" x 4½" Fabric B piece as shown. Press. Make two, one of each variation.

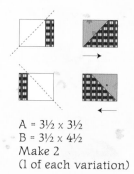

A = 3½ x 3½
B = 3½ x 4½
Make 2
(1 of each variation)

6. Sew two 4½" x 10½" Fabric A pieces to units from step 5 as shown. Press.

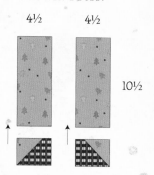

7. Sew 1½" x 8½" Fabric A piece and units from step 2 and 4 together as shown. Press. Sew this unit between units from step 6. Press.

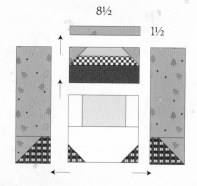

8. Refer to photo on page 6 and layout on page 12 to embroider or quick-fuse appliqué the word WELCOME to 12" x 8" piece of Fabric G. Use a font on your embroidery machine, or satin stitch by hand using the template on page 13 and Embroidery Stitch Guide on page 108.

Or, refer to Quick-Fuse Appliqué on page 109. Trace, position, and fuse WELCOME to 12" x 8" Fabric G piece. Finish edges with decorative stitching as desired.

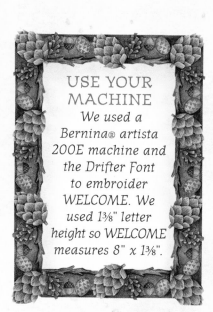

USE YOUR MACHINE
We used a Bernina® artista 200E machine and the Drifter Font to embroider WELCOME. We used 1⅜" letter height so WELCOME measures 8" x 1⅜".

9. Trim Fabric G piece from step 8 to 10½" x 4". Sew between two 4" x 3½" Fabric B pieces as shown. Press.

10. Sew 11½" x 4½" Fabric H piece to 1" x 11½" Fabric B piece as shown. Press. Sew unit between two 5" x 3" Fabric B pieces as shown. Press.

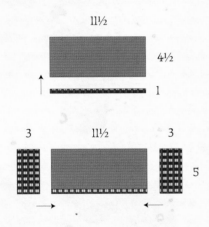

11. Making quick corner triangle units, sew two 1½" Fabric A squares to unit from step 10 as shown. Press.

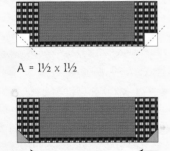

A = 1½ x 1½

12. Sew units from steps 7, 9, and 11 together as shown. Press. Sew unit between two 2½" x 21½" Fabric A pieces as shown. Press.

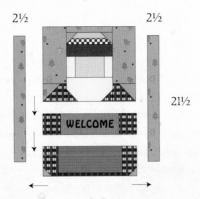

13. Sew 5½" x 14½" Fabric B piece between two 3½" x 5½" Fabric A pieces as shown. Press.

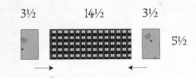

14. Sew 2½" x 11½" Fabric F piece between 8½" x 11½" Fabric C piece and 1½" x 11½" Fabric D piece as shown. Press.

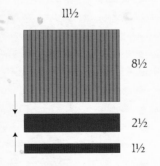

We almost always have snow in time for Christmas. No matter how hectic the holidays seem to be, we make time to play in the snow.

15. Sew unit from step 14 between two 5" x 11½" Fabric A pieces as shown. Press.

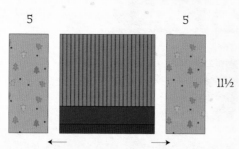

16. Making quick corner triangle units, sew two 1½" Fabric A squares to 3" x 18½" Fabric D piece as shown. Press.

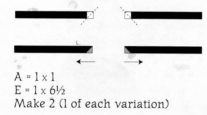

A = 1½ x 1½
D = 3 x 18½

17. Making quick corner triangle units, sew 1" Fabric A square to 1" x 6½" Fabric E piece as shown. Make two, one of each variation. Press.

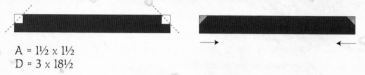

A = 1 x 1
E = 1 x 6½
Make 2 (1 of each variation)

18. Sew 1" x 6½" Fabric E piece between units from step 17 as shown. Press.

19. Sew unit from step 16 to unit from step 18 as shown. Press. Sew unit between two 1½" x 3½" Fabric A pieces as shown. Press.

20. Sew unit from step 15 between units from steps 13 and 19 as shown. Press. Referring to photo on page 6 and layout on page 12, sew this unit to unit from step 12. Press.

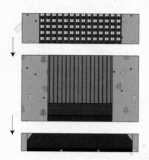

Adding the Appliqués and Embellishments

1. Refer to Quick-Fuse Appliqué directions on page 109. Trace appliqué patterns on page 13 for moustache, eyebrow, mitten, and cuff.

2. Referring to photo on page 6 and layout on page 12, position appliqués on center panel. Fuse appliqués in place and finish with machine satin stitch or decorative stitching as desired.

3. Referring to Embroidery Stitch Guide on page 108, Moustache Template on page 13, and photo on page 6, use two strands of embroidery floss and a stem stitch to embroider nose.

Borders

Refer to Accurate Seam Allowance on page 108 prior to piecing border.

1. Making quick corner triangle units, sew 2½" Fabric N square to 2½" Fabric O square as shown. Press. Make sixty.

N = 2½ x 2½
O = 2½ x 2½
Make 60

2. Sew ten units from step 1 together as shown. Press. Sew unit to 2½" x 20½" Fabric N piece as shown. Press. Make two.

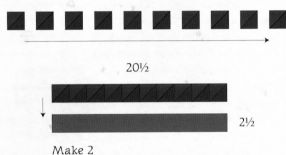

20½

2½

Make 2

3. Referring to photo on page 6 and layout on page 12, sew units from step 2 to top and bottom of center panel. Press seams toward borders.

4. Referring to photo on page 6 and layout on page 12, sew twenty units from step 1 together. Press. Make two. Sew one unit to 2½" x 40½" Fabric N strip. Press. Make two.

Woodland Welcome Door Decoration

Welcome family and friends with a basket filled with greenery on the door.

This colorful door decoration combines fresh greenery, crabapples, berries, and twigs in a rustic woven basket. The brightly colored crabapples contrast beautifully with the lush mixture of woodland greenery. Bare sticks and berries add texture and interest to the arrangement. Look for a narrow, rectangular basket that will hang relatively flat on the door.

Hang the basket on the door and fill with an assortment of fresh greenery, using the photo as a guide for shape. Then, add real or faux twigs, crabapples, and berries. Cut greenery will last for several weeks outdoors in cold climates so it is not necessary to place the greenery in water. If you live in a warm climate, you may wish to line your basket with plastic then fill it with water-soaked florist foam before beginning your arrangement.

5. Draw diagonal line on wrong side of 5" Fabric N square. Place marked square on 5" Fabric O square, right sides together. Sew a scant ¼" away from drawn line on both sides to make half-square triangles. Make two. Cut on drawn line and press. Square units to 4½". This will make four half-square triangles.

N = 5 x 5
O = 5 x 5
Make 2

Square to 4½
Make 4

6. Referring to photo on page 6 and layout, sew a unit from step 5 to each end of border unit from step 4. Press. Make two. Sew units to sides of quilt. Press seams toward borders.

ADD ROSY CHEEKS
Use blush to give Santa a rosy glow!

Layering and Finishing

1. Trim backing to make one 33" x 53" (approximate) backing piece. Arrange and baste backing, batting, and top together, referring to Layering the Quilt on page 111. Hand or machine quilt as desired. Use perle cotton and stem stitch to embroider lines on the coat, pants, and boots. Use perle cotton and Big Stitch Quilting Technique on page 111 to quilt arms.

2. Referring to photo on page 6 and layout for placement, sew two ⅜" buttons for eyes and two 1" buttons on coat. Sew pom-pom to hat.

3. Sew 2¾" x 42" binding strips end-to-end to make one continuous 2¾"-wide strip. Refer to Binding the Quilt on page 111 and bind quilt to finish.

4. Use two 12" lengths of perle cotton to stitch on shoe laces and tie in a bow.

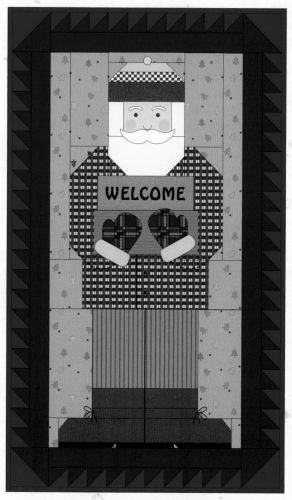

Timberland Santa Door Banner
Finished Size: 29" x 49"
Photo: page 6

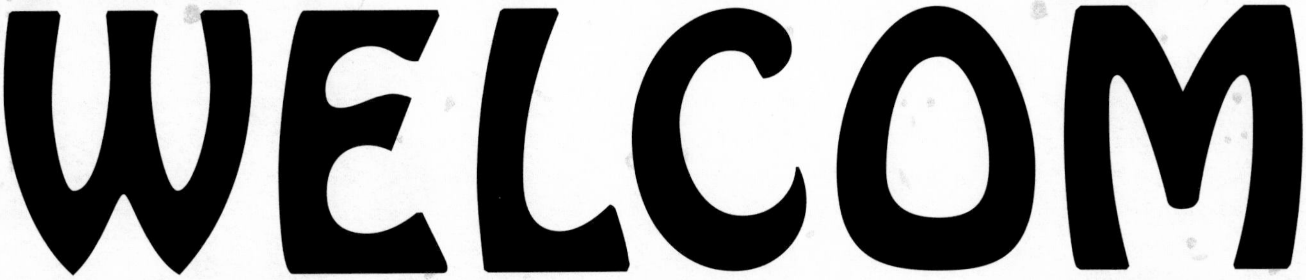

WELCOM

Welcome Letters
Reverse for Quick-Fuse Appliqué.

**Timberland Santa Door Banner
Quick-Fuse Appliqué Templates**
(page 109)

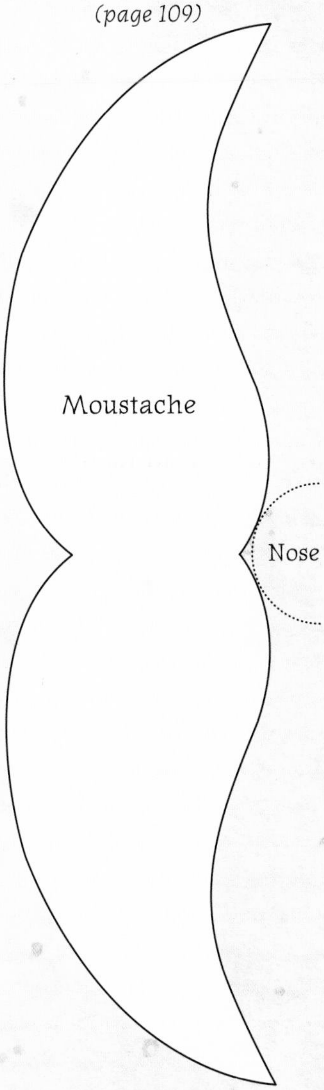

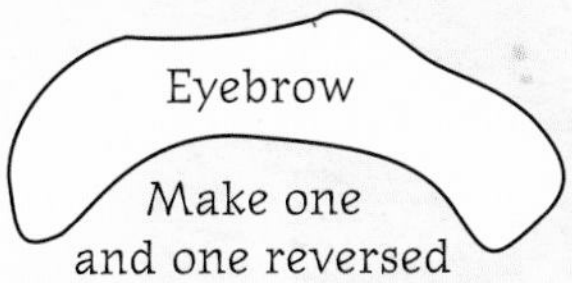

Moustache

Nose

Mitten and Cuff
Make one and one reversed

Eyebrow

Make one
and one reversed

Tracing Line _____
Tracing Line - - - - - - -
(will be hidden behind other fabric)
Embroidery Line ....

Winter Woods Bed Quilt

Finished size: 67" x 91"

My home is in Spokane, Washington, which is located in the middle of a ponderosa pine forest. Gigantic trees surround my studio and the nearby mountains are carpeted with luxurious green pine growth. It's a pleasure to look out my studio window and see pine trees everywhere. I tried to capture that beauty in this quilt project that uses an ingenious technique to make two quilts at the same time.

Fabric Requirements and Cutting Instructions

Read all instructions before beginning and use ¼"-wide seam allowances throughout. Read Cutting Strips and Pieces on page 108 prior to cutting fabrics.

Winter Woods Bed Quilt 67" x 91" and Miniature Blocks	FIRST CUT		SECOND CUT	
	Number of Strips or Pieces	Dimensions	Number of Pieces	Dimensions
Fabric A Large Tree Background 1⅛ yards	1	20½" x 42"	1	20½" square
	4	4½" x 42"	33	4½" squares
			1	2½" square
Fabric B Small Tree Background 1 yard	1	9½" x 42"	4	9½" squares
	6	3½" x 42"	60	3½" squares
			4	2" squares
Fabric C Large Tree ⅝ yard	1	20½" x 42"	1	20½" square
Fabric D Small Trees ⅓ yard each of four fabrics	1*	9½" square	*cut for each fabric	
Fabric E Branches *Nine assorted fabrics to total* 1½ yards	38	4½" squares		
	60	3½" squares		
	6	2½" squares		
	4	2" squares		
Fabric F Large Tree Trunks ⅙ yard	1	4½" x 42"	1	4½" x 15"
			1	2½" x 7¾"
Fabric G Small Tree Trunks ¼ yard	1	7½" x 42"	4	7½" x 2½"
			4	4" x 1½"
Fabric H Side Setting and Corner Setting Triangles 1½ yards	2	25⅜" x 42"	2	25⅜" squares *(cut twice diagonally)*
			2	13" squares *(cut once diagonally)*
BED QUILT BORDERS				
Large Tree Accent Border and Second Border ¾ yard	7	2½" x 42"		
	4	1½" x 42"	2	1½" x 34½"
			2	1½" x 32½"
Small Tree Accent Border ½ yard	8	1½" x 42"	8	1½" x 17½"
			8	1½" x 15½"

Winter Woods Bed Quilt Borders Continued	FIRST CUT	
	Number of Strips	Dimensions
First Border ⅜ yard	7	1½" x 42"
Outside Border 1½ yards	8	6½" x 42"
Binding ⅔ yard	8	2¾" x 42"

Backing - 5½ yards
Batting - 75" x 99"
Lightweight Fusible Web - ⅝ yard (optional)

Making the Quilt

You will be making five tree blocks, one large and four smaller blocks for the bed quilt, and five miniature blocks for a table or wall quilt at the same time. A Dual Quick Corner Triangle technique is used as described in step one. This technique adds a twist to traditional Quick Corner Triangles by making two units at one time.

Making the Large Tree Blocks

Whenever possible, use the Assembly Line Method on page 108. Press seams in direction of arrows. Refer to Accurate Seam Allowance on page 108 prior to sewing.

1. To make Dual Quick Corner Triangles, draw a diagonal line through center of 4½" Fabric A square. Draw a second diagonal line ½" away from first drawn line, on one side only. Place marked square, right sides together on 4½" Fabric E square. Sew on first drawn line then second drawn line. Cut units apart between stitched lines. Press. This will make one 4½" unit and one smaller unit. <u>Square smaller unit to 2½"</u>. Repeat to make thirty-two 4½" triangle squares and thirty-two 2½" triangle squares.

Fabric A = 4½ x 4½
Fabric E = 4½ x 4½

Make 32   Make 32
Square to 4½"   Square to 2½"

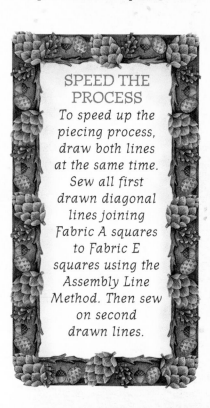
2. Arrange thirteen 4½" units from step 1 and two 4½" Fabric E squares to make three rows, as shown. Sew units together to make rows. Press. Sew rows together. Press. Repeat using thirteen 2½" units and two 2½" Fabric E squares to make miniature block.

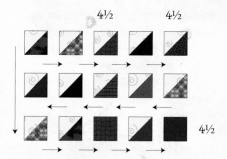

4½   4½

4½

3. Arrange nineteen 4½" units from step 1, four 4½" Fabric E squares, and one 4½" Fabric A square to make three rows as shown. Sew units together to make rows. Press. Sew rows together. Press. Repeat for miniature block, using nineteen 2½" units, four 2½" Fabric E squares, and one 2½" Fabric A square. Press.

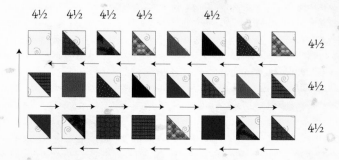

4½   4½   4½   4½   4½

4½

4½

4½

4. Referring to Dual Quick Corner Triangles in step 1, mark and sew 20½" Fabric A square to 20½" Fabric C square, as shown. Cut unit apart between stitched lines. Press. Trim and square smaller unit to 10½" for miniature block.

Fabric A = 20½ x 20½   Square to   Square to
Fabric C = 20½ x 20½   20½" x 20½"   10½" x 10½"

5. Referring to Hand Appliqué on page 109, appliqué 4½" x 15" Fabric F strip to 20½" unit from step 4, as shown. Trim as needed. Repeat for miniature block, using 2½" x 7¾" Fabric F strip and 10½" unit from step 4.

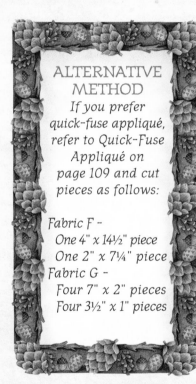

6. Sew units from steps 2, 3, and 5 together as shown. Press. Repeat for miniature block.

Large Block measures 32½" x 32½"
Miniature Block measures 16½" x 16½"

Making the Small Tree Blocks

1. Make Dual Quick Corner Triangles by drawing two diagonal lines ½" apart on wrong side of 3½" Fabric B square, as shown. Place marked 3½" Fabric B square on 3½" Fabric E square, right sides together. Sew on drawn lines. Cut units apart between stitched lines as shown. Press. Make fifty-six 3½" units. Trim and square smaller fifty-six units to 2" for miniature blocks.

Fabric B = 3½ x 3½
Fabric E = 3½ x 3½
Make 56 - 3½" squares
Make 56 - 2" squares

2. Arrange six 3½" units from step 1 to make two rows, as shown. Sew units into rows. Press. Sew rows together. Press. Make four. Repeat to make four miniature blocks, using 2" units.

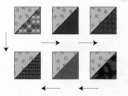

Make 4 of each size

3. Arrange eight 3½" units from step 1, 3½" Fabric B square, and 3½" Fabric E square as shown to make two rows. Sew units into rows. Press. Sew rows together. Press. Make four. Repeat to make four miniature blocks, using 2" units, 2" Fabric B squares and 2" Fabric E squares.

3½   3½

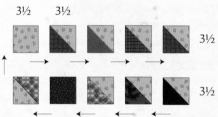

3½

3½

Make 4 of each size

4. Referring to Dual Quick Corner Triangles in step 1, mark and sew 9½" Fabric B square to 9½" Fabric D square, as shown. Cut units apart between stitched lines. Press. Make four 9½" units. Trim and square smaller units to 5". Make four for miniature blocks.

B = 9½ x 9½
D = 9½ x 9½

Make 4
Square to 9½"

Make 4
Square to 5"

5. Referring to Hand Appliqué on page 109, appliqué 7½" x 2½" Fabric G strip to 9½" unit from step 4. Make four. Press. Repeat for miniature blocks, using 4" x 1½" Fabric G strip. Make four.

6. Sew units from steps 2, 3, and 5 together as shown. Press. Make four Small Tree Blocks for bed quilt. Make four Miniature Small Tree Blocks.

Make 4 of each size
Block measures 15½" x 15½"
Miniature Block measures 8" x 8"

Set aside miniature blocks for use in a table quilt or wall quilt. Directions begin on page 20.

Making Bed Quilt

1. Referring to photo on page 14 and layout on page 20, sew two 1½" x 32½" Large Tree Accent Border strips to opposite sides of 32½" Large Tree Block. Press. Sew two 1½" x 34½" Large Tree Accent Border strips to remaining sides of block. Press.

2. Referring to photo on page 14 and layout on page 20, sew two 1½" x 15½" Small Tree Accent Border strips to opposite sides of 15½" Small Tree Block. Press. Sew two 1½" x 17½" Small Tree Accent border strips to remaining sides of Small Tree Block. Press. Make four.

Snowshoeing is a popular pastime in the mountains around here. With snacks in a pack and poles for balance, you can go just about anywhere.

Assembly

1. Sew Small Tree Block between Fabric H corner setting triangle and side setting triangle as shown. Press. Make two, one of each variation. Press.

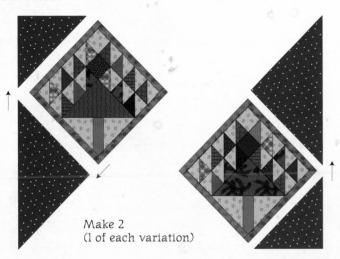

Make 2
(1 of each variation)

2. Sew Small Tree Block between Fabric H corner setting triangle and two side setting triangles as shown. Make two, one of each variation. Press.

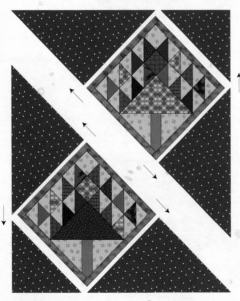

Make 2
(1 of each variation)

3. Referring to photo on page 14 and layout on page 20, sew units from step 1 to opposite sides of large tree block. Press.

4. Referring to photo on page 14 and layout on page 20, sew units from step 2 to remaining sides of large tree block. Press.

Borders

1. Sew 1½" x 42" First Border strips end-to-end to make one continuous 1½"-wide strip. Referring to Adding the Borders on page 110, measure quilt through center from side to side. Cut two 1½"-wide First Border strips to that measurement. Sew to top and bottom of quilt. Press seams toward borders.

2. Measure quilt through center from top to bottom, including borders just added. Cut two 1½"-wide First Border strips to that measurement. Sew to sides of quilt. Press seams toward borders.

3. Repeat steps 1 and 2 to join, fit, trim, and sew 2½"-wide Second Border strips and 6½"-wide Outside Border strips to top, bottom, and sides of quilt. Press seams toward borders.

Layering and Binding

1. Cut backing crosswise into two equal pieces. Sew pieces together to make one 83" x 99" (approximate) backing piece. Press. Cut backing to 75" x 99". Arrange and baste backing, batting, and top together, referring to Layering the Quilt on page 111.

2. Hand or machine quilt as desired.

3. Sew 2¾" x 42" binding strips end-to-end to make one continuous 2¾"-wide strip. Refer to Binding the Quilt on page 111 and bind quilt to finish.

Winter Woods Table or Wall Quilt

Finished size: 36" x 36"

*Life is busy, so I love it when
I can do two projects at once!
With Dual Quick Corner Triangles,
blocks for the Winter Woods Bed Quilt
and this smaller quilt are
made at the same time.*

Winter Woods Table or Wall Quilt 36" x 36"	FIRST CUT	
	Number of Strips or Pieces	Dimensions
Miniature Blocks from Winter Woods Bed Quilt		
Fabric A Background Border ½ yard	4	8" x 16½"
Accent Border ½ yard	4	1½" x 35½"
	4	1½" x 16½"
	8	1½" x 8"
Binding ⅜ yard	4	2¾" x 42"
Backing - 1¼ yards Batting - 43" x 43"		

Making the Table or Wall Quilt

Use a simple border treatment and the Miniature Blocks constructed in Winter Woods Bed Quilt, pages 15-18, to create a woodland accent for any room.

Winter Woods Bed Quilt
Finished Size: 67" x 91"
Photo: page 14

1. Sew 8" x 16½" Fabric A strip between two 1½" x 16½" Accent Border strips. Press. Make two.

2. Sew Miniature Large Tree Block between two units from step 1. Press.

3. Referring to photo, sew unit from step 2 between two 1½" x 35½" Accent Border strips. Press.

4. Sew four 1½" x 8" Accent Border pieces, two Small Tree Blocks, and one 8" x 16½" Fabric A strip together as shown. Press. Make two. If desired, all the Small Tree Blocks can be oriented in the same upright direction for the Winter Woods Wall Quilt Variation shown at top right.

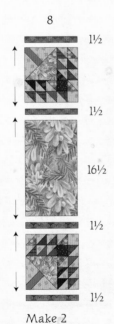

8

1½

1½

16½

1½

1½

Make 2

5. Referring to photo or layout, sew unit from step 3 between two units from step 4. Press.

6. Referring to photo, sew remaining 1½" x 35½" strips to sides of quilt.

7. Arrange and baste backing, batting, and top together referring to Layering the Quilt on page 111. Hand or machine quilt as desired.

8. Refer to Binding the Quilt on page 111 and bind quilt to finish.

Winter Woods Wall Quilt
Variation

Winter Woods Table or Wall Quilt
Finished Size: 36" x 36"

Holiday Mountain Sled

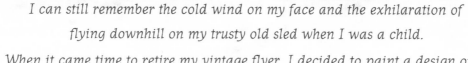

I can still remember the cold wind on my face and the exhilaration of flying downhill on my trusty old sled when I was a child.

When it came time to retire my vintage flyer, I decided to paint a design on it so it could decorate the porch, sparking memories of those fun days in the snow.

Materials Needed:

Sled

Acrylic paints in ivory, tan, red, black, brown, medium green, and dark green

Assorted paintbrushes

Sandpaper - fine grit

Sea sponge

Crackle medium

Matte spray varnish

Decorative cord *(Optional)*

Tracing paper

Graphite transfer paper

Antiquing medium *(Optional)*

Miracle Sponge™

* Miracle Sponge is thinly compressed cellulose that expands when wet. It is available at many art and craft supply stores.

Painting the Sled

Refer to photo for guidance as needed. Allow paint to dry thoroughly between each step.

1. Sand off any existing varnish on sled. To provide a rustic look, do not seal the wood before painting.

2. Basecoat center slat and steering bar with black acrylic paint. Basecoat side slats with ivory paint and wood trim over runners with dark green paint. Allow to dry thoroughly.

3. Following manufacturer's directions, apply crackle medium to center slat and steering bar. Allow to "set" according to manufacturer's specifications.

4. Apply a quick, even coat of red paint to the center slat and steering bar. Crackles will appear in the painted surface. Do not touch as surface is very fragile when wet. Dry thoroughly. Sand edges for a rustic look.

5. Dampen sea sponge with water and wring thoroughly. Dip sponge in ivory paint then tan paint. Blot on a paper towel. Using a tapping motion, sponge color onto side slats, applying lightly for a mottled effect. Sponge a little more tan toward the edges of the slats to deepen the color. When dry, sand edges.

6. Using template below and tracing paper, make a full length template of bough and cone motif. Repeat tracing the motif, alternating between original and reverse images, connecting where shown, to make a template the appropriate length for your sled. We used four original and four reversed images for our template. You may need to adjust the size of the motif and the number of repeats based on the size of your sled. Transfer painting template to the sponged side slats using graphite transfer paper.

7. Paint motif using brown for the stem and medium green for the needles. Trace pinecone shape onto Miracle Sponge™. Cut out with craft scissors and dip in water to expand. Wring thoroughly. Dip pinecone-shaped sponge in brown paint, blot on paper towel, and sponge cones on sled where indicated, redipping sponge as needed. Dry thoroughly. Sand over design lightly.

8. Spray with several coats of matte spray varnish following manufacturer's directions. If desired, apply antiquing medium over entire surface, following manufacturer's directions for application and finishing.

9. Add decorative cording to steering bar if desired.

Holiday Mountain
Sled Vine Template

Mountain Lodge Luminarias

As dusk appears, there is nothing quite as welcoming
as the glow of candlelight on the snow. I love to set out these lanterns
to welcome my wintertime guests. Woodland creatures and holiday motifs
are outlined in the tiny points of light.

Materials Needed

38 Gauge aluminum tooling foil
(Available at art supply stores)
Large nail
Paper punch
Ruler and pencil
Leather lacing
Brass plated round head
   paper fasteners
Quart canning jars
Sand
Candles to fit inside canning jars
Matboard or foam core
Scissors

Making the Luminarias

1. Our foil came in a roll 12" wide by 36" long. Foil is goldtone on one side and silver on the other. Using scissors, cut foil into two 12" x 18" pieces.

2. Use a ruler to measure and mark lines 1" from edge along both sides of 12" length. Fold foil over at the line. Refer to photo for guidance.
   Note: keeping the gold color on the inside of the luminarias will make a soft golden glow when lit. Silver on the inside will cause a brighter, colder light.

3. Use ruler to measure and mark lacing hole placement in upper and lower gold borders. Space holes 2" apart and ¼" from edge of border. Holes are also spaced 2" apart on lower portion of same border, but are offset 1" from the holes along outside edge. Use a paper punch to punch holes.

4. Copy your choice of Forest Friends Templates on pages 37-39 or Snowflake Templates on pages 86 and 96, and Pinecone and Pine Bough Templates on page 47. Keeping foil flat, tape paper pattern onto foil centering between the borders and spacing as desired. Place foil on matboard or foam core with an old board underneath. Following the lines on your paper pattern, use a large nail to pierce the foil outlining the motif and spacing holes evenly.

5. Roll foil into a cylinder shape. It is easier to shape the foil by rolling it around a large can such as a 3 lb. coffee can. Use round head paper fasteners to hold the ends together.

6. Lace leather strips through the holes in the border, tying the ends together to finish.

7. Place candle in 2"-3" of sand in the canning jar and insert inside foil luminaria. Light the candle and enjoy your welcoming candlelight.
   Note: never leave burning candles unattended.

Snowflakes drift softly through the twilight sky. Cross-country skiers swoosh by, barely making a sound in the forest stillness. The winter-blue mountains are decked with garlands of pines and a frosting of new-fallen snow. In the cabin, the family gathers to sing Christmas carols by the fire. It's time for a holiday in the pines.

Holiday in the Pines

Cozy Lodge Quilt

Finished size: 75" x 104"

What could be cozier than curling up in this colorful quilt and relaxing in front of a warm fire? I love to relax by the fireplace, sip tea, and watch a favorite movie. The warm colors and geometric pattern of this quilt remind me of the Northwest's Native American heritage. The strip-piecing method makes this variation of a Bargello quilt much easier than it looks.

Fabric Requirements and Cutting Instructions

Read all instructions before beginning and use ¼"-wide seam allowances throughout. Read Cutting Strips and Pieces on page 108 prior to cutting fabrics.

Cozy Lodge Bed Quilt 75" x 104"	FIRST CUT	
	Number of Strips or Pieces	Dimensions
Fabric A Strips and Pieced Border 2⅓ yards	22	3½" x 42"
Fabrics B, C, D, E, F, G and H Strips and Pieced Border 1⅙ yards each of seven fabrics **	11*	3½" x 42" *cut for each fabric
BORDERS		
First Border	8	3½" x 42"
Second Border ½ yard	8	1½" x 42"
Fourth Border ½ yard	8	2" x 42"
Outside Border 1¼ yards	9	4½" x 42"
Binding ¾ yard	9	2¾" x 42"
Backing - 7 yards Batting - 83" x 112"		
**We used 2 golds, 2 greens, 2 reds, and 1 black.		

Making the Blocks

You will be making twelve Bargello Blocks. Blocks measure 26½" x 14" unfinished. There will be leftover pieced segments. These are incorporated into the Third Border and used for the Cozy Lodge Stockings on page 52. Segments can also be used for a scrappy binding or pillow. Whenever possible, use the Assembly Line Method on page 108. Press all seams in same direction. Refer to Accurate Seam Allowance on page 108 prior to sewing.

Bargello Blocks

1. Sew together 3½" x 42" Fabric A, B, C, D, E, F, A, G, and H strips as shown. Press. Make eleven strip sets.

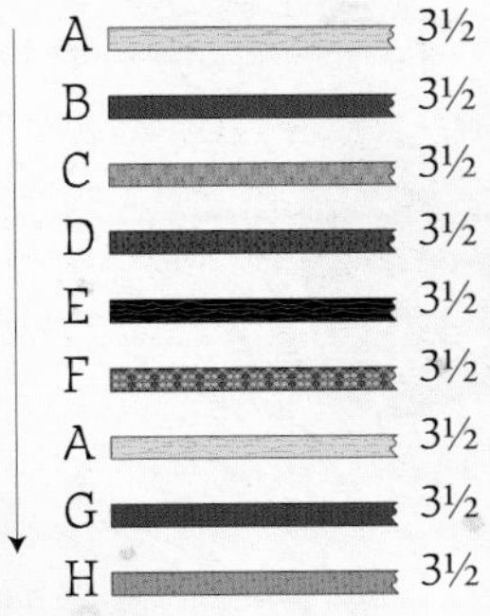

```
A ─────────  3½
B ─────────  3½
C ─────────  3½
D ─────────  3½
E ─────────  3½
F ─────────  3½
A ─────────  3½
G ─────────  3½
H ─────────  3½
```

Make 11

2. From strip sets, cut sixty 2½"-wide segments, ninety-six 2"-wide segments, and forty-eight 1½"-wide segments.

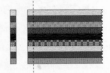

Cut sixty 2½" segments
Ninety-six 2" segments
Forty-eight 1½" segments

3. Arrange seventeen segments from step 2 for one Bargello Block as shown. Using a seam ripper, remove stitches at seams as shown. Segments for the block are now 15½" long. Press ends flat where stitches were removed. Set aside unused portions to be used later for pieced border. To speed the process, stack twelve matching segments together, then remove stitches where indicated for each stack.

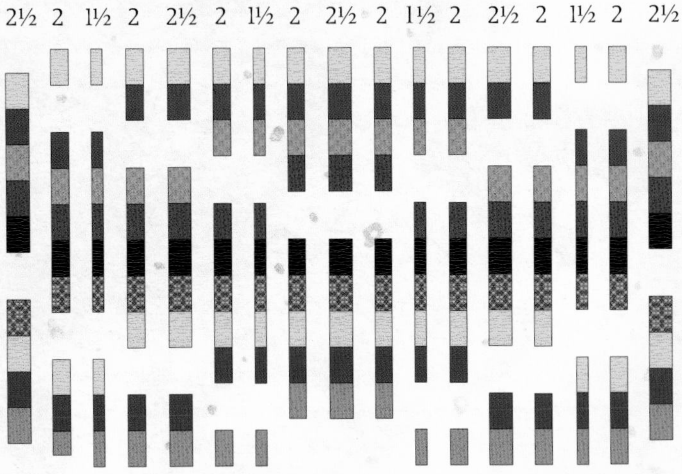

2½ 2 1½ 2 2½ 2 1½ 2 2½ 2 1½ 2 2½ 2 1½ 2 2½

Make 12

4. To align adjacent segments accurately for piecing, cut notches at center of every third segment on odd rows and second and fourth segments on even rows. Take care to cut only in edge of seam allowance. Match notches to seams in neighboring segments as shown. For example, fold third section Fabric C piece in half and cut a tiny notch at the midpoint on both sides, staying inside the ¼"-wide seam allowance. Align notches with seams between Fabric C and D pieces on adjacent segments.

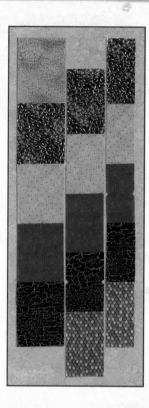

5. Sew segments together as shown. Press. Trim to 26½" x 14". Make twelve Bargello Blocks.

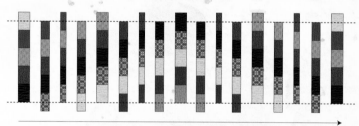

Make 12

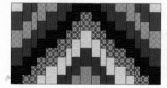

Block measures 26½" x 14"
Make 12

Assembly

1. Refer to photo on page 28 and layout. Arrange and sew blocks in six horizontal rows of two blocks each. Press.

2. Arrange rows, reversing orientation of every other row as shown on layout.

3. Sew rows together. Press. Quilt top measures 52½" x 81½".

Borders

1. Sew 3½" x 42" First Border strips end-to-end to make one continuous 3½"-wide strip. Referring to Adding the Borders on page 110, measure quilt through center from side to side. Cut two 3½"-wide First Border strips to that measurement. Sew to top and bottom of quilt. Press toward borders.

2. Measure quilt through center from top to bottom, including borders just added. Cut two 3½"-wide First Border strips to that measurement. Sew to sides of quilt. Press.

3. Repeat steps 1 and 2 to fit, trim, and sew 1½"-wide Second Border strips to top, bottom, and sides of quilt. Press seams toward borders. Measure width and length of quilt top. Use these measurements in steps 4 and 5.

4. To make pieced border, use 2"-wide leftover segments, from step 3 in Making the Blocks, and trim 2½"-wide segments to 2"-wide. Referring to quilt layout, arrange and sew together enough 2"-wide segments to equal width of quilt top. Make two. Press. Sew pieced borders to top and bottom of quilt. Press toward Second Border.

5. Repeat step 4 to join 2"-wide segments to equal length of quilt top as measured in step 3, trim as needed. Add 2" square to each end of pieced border. Press. Make two. Sew to sides of quilt. Press toward Second Border.

6. Repeat steps 1 and 2 to join, fit, trim, and sew 2"-wide Fourth Border strips and 4½"-wide Outside Border strips to top, bottom, and sides of quilt. Press.

Layering and Binding

1. Cut backing fabric crosswise into three equal pieces. Sew pieces together to make one 83" x 125" (approximate) backing piece. Press. Cut backing to 83" x 112". Arrange and baste backing, batting, and top together, referring to Layering the Quilt on page 111.

2. Hand or machine quilt as desired.

3. Sew 2¾" x 42" binding strips end-to-end to make one continuous 2¾"-wide strip. Refer to Binding the Quilt on page 111 and bind quilt to finish.

Cozy Lodge Quilt
Finished Size: 75" x 104"
Photo: page 28

Rustic Twig Ornaments

Celebrate those fun family activities outdoors by using twigs to frame your favorite photos! Perfect to hang on the tree or give as gifts, these rustic twig frames will be a reminder of special times together.

Materials Needed
Matboard
Color photocopies of favorite snapshots
 OR duplicate copies of your snapshots
Twigs, moss, and other natural elements
Hot glue gun and glue sticks
Cording, faux holly, and other embellishments
Double-stick tape

For each ornament, cut two matching pieces of matboard to your choice of size. If core of matboard is white, use a black permanent marker to color edges of matboard black. Mount photo on one piece of matboard in the position desired using double-stick tape. Arrange and glue twigs in your choice of pattern around the photo. Use pruning shears to cut twigs to size.

Decorate the twig frames with cording, moss, holly, and other dried natural elements. Attach a hanging cord to the back of frame using tape or hot glue. Affix matching piece of matboard to the back with colored side out to finish ornament.

Forest Friends
Wall Quilt

Finished size: 69" x 49"

A moose wandered into town recently and made quite a stir at the hardware store. We often see deer on the outskirts of town and on the way to work one day, I even saw a coyote. One of the things I love about the Northwest is our close proximity to wildlife. We pay tribute to these magnificent animals in this striking wall quilt. Forest animals are silhouetted and framed against a woodland glade background of richly colored flannels.

Fabric Requirements and Cutting Instructions

Read all instructions before beginning and use ¼"-wide seam allowances throughout. Read Cutting Strips and Pieces on page 108 prior to cutting fabrics.

Forest Friends Wall Quilt 69" x 49"	FIRST CUT		SECOND CUT	
	Number of Strips or Pieces	Dimensions	Number of Pieces	Dimensions
Fabric A Background ¼ yard	2	3" x 42"	24	3" squares
Fabric B Triangles 1 yard	10	3" x 42"	24	3" x 5½"
			72	3" squares
Fabric C Accent Square 1 yard	6	5½" x 42"	24	5½" squares
			24	5½" x 3"
Fabric D Silhouette Background and Triangles 1 yard	3	5½" x 42"	6	5½" x 9½"
			12	5½" x 2½"
	2	3" x 42"	24	3" squares
	3	2½" x 42"	24	2½" squares
			24	2½" x 2"
Fabric E Background ⅞ yard	9	3" x 42"	24	3" x 8"
			24	3" x 5½"
Fabric F Center Accent ½ yard	7	2" x 42"	24	2" x 5½"
			48	2" squares
BORDERS				
First Border ⅓ yard	6	1½" x 42"		
Outside Border 2⅛ yards* OR ¾ yard (non-directional)	2	72½" x 3½"		
	2	52½" x 3½"		
Binding ⅝ yard	6	2¾" x 42"		

Silhouette Appliqués - ½ yard
Lightweight Fusible Web - ¾ yard
Backing - 3⅛ yards
Batting - 75" x 55"
We used a border print for our border, the yardage may vary with border prints depending on the number of repeats in the fabric.

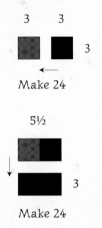

Making the Blocks

You will be making six Silhouette Blocks. Blocks measure 20½" square unfinished. Whenever possible, use the Assembly Line Method on page 108. Press seams in direction of arrows.

Silhouette Blocks

1. Sew 3" Fabric A square to 3" Fabric B square as shown. Press. Make twenty-four. Sew 3" x 5½" Fabric B piece to unit as shown. Press. Make twenty-four.

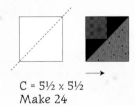

Make 24

Make 24

2. Refer to Quick Corner Triangles on page 108. Sew 5½" Fabric C square to unit from step 1 as shown. Press. Make twenty-four.

C = 5½ x 5½
Make 24

3. Making a quick corner triangle unit, sew 2½" Fabric D square to unit from step 2 as shown. Press. Make twenty-four.

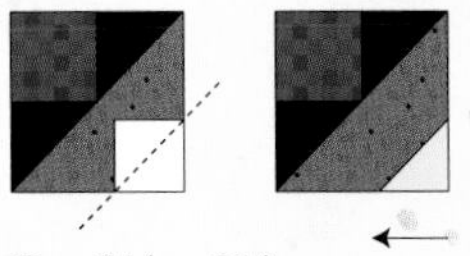

D = 2½ x 2½
Make 24

4. Making a quick corner triangle unit, sew 3" Fabric D square to 3" x 8" Fabric E piece as shown. Press. Make twenty-four, pressing twelve seams in opposite direction.

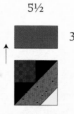

D = 3 x 3
E = 3 x 8
Make 24

5. Sew 3" x 5½" Fabric E piece to unit from step 3 as shown. Press. Make twenty-four. Sew this unit to unit from step 4 as shown. Press. Make twenty-four.

Make 24

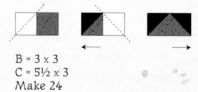

Make 24

6. Making quick corner triangle units, sew two 3" Fabric B squares to 5½" x 3" Fabric C piece as shown. Press. Make twenty-four.

B = 3 x 3
C = 5½ x 3
Make 24

7. Sew 2½" x 2" Fabric D piece between two 2" Fabric F squares as shown. Press. Make twenty-four.

2   2½   2

2

Make 24

8. Sew 2" x 5½" Fabric F piece between unit from step 6 and unit from step 7 as shown. Press. Make twenty-four.

5½

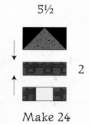
2

Make 24

9. Sew 5½" x 2½" Fabric D piece to unit from step 8 as shown. Press. Make twelve. Sew this unit between two units from step 5 as shown. Press. Make twelve.

5½

2½

Make 12

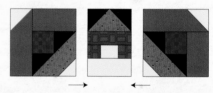

Make 12

During the winter, moose and deer move closer to town while looking for winter forage. It is a real thrill to see these magnificent creatures so close to home.

10. Sew 5½" x 9½" Fabric D piece between two units from step 8 as shown. Press. Make six.

5½

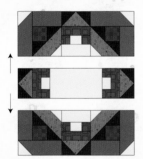

9½

Make 6

11. Sew unit from step 10 between two units from step 9 as shown. Press. Make six. Block measures 20½" square.

Make 6
Block measures 20½"

Finished Size: 16" x 16"

Moose on the Loose Pillow

A friendly moose will wander into your home and heart on this charming pillow. Adapted from the Forest Friends Quilt, this pillow is the perfect accent for lodge décor. If desired, use strip-pieced scraps from the Cozy Lodge Quilt to make the back so you can flip the pillow over for a completely different look.

Materials Needed

Fabric A Block Corner - Scrap
  Four 3" squares
Fabric B Triangles - ⅛ yard
  Four 3" x 5½" pieces
  Four 3" squares
Fabric C Accent Square - ¼ yard
  Four 5½" squares
Fabric D Silhouette Background and Accent Border - ⅛ yard
  Four 2½" squares
  Two 1" x 11½" pieces
  Two 1" x 10½" pieces
Outside Border - ⅝ yard directional
  Four 21" x 3" strips
Moose Appliqué - Scrap
Lining and Batting - ⅝ yard
  20" square of each
Pillow Backing - ½ yard
  Two 11" x 16½" pieces

Making the Pillow

1. Sew 3" Fabric A square to 3" Fabric B square as shown. Press. Make 4. Sew unit to 3" x 5½" Fabric B piece as shown. Press. Make four.

3   3   5½
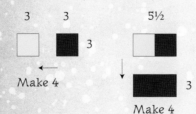
Make 4   Make 4

2. Refer to Quick Corner Triangles on page 108. Sew 5½" Fabric C square to unit from step 1 as shown. Press. Make four. Press two in opposite direction.

C = 5½ x 5½
Make 4

3. Making a quick corner triangle unit, sew 2½" Fabric D square to unit from step 2 as shown. Press. Make four. Press two in opposite direction.

D = 2½ x 2½
Make 4

4. Referring to photo, arrange and sew units from step 3 together. Press.

5. Sew unit from step 4 between two 1" x 10½" Accent Border pieces. Press. Sew this unit between two 1" x 11½" Accent Border pieces.

6. Refer to Mitered Borders on page 110. Sew Outside Border strips to pillow top on all four sides, mitering corners. Press.

7. Refer to Quick-Fuse Appliqué on page 109 and Moose Ornament Template on page 55 to appliqué silhouette.

8. Refer to Finishing Pillows on page 111 to quilt top, sew backing piece to pillow, and make pillow form.

Adding the Appliqués

The instructions given are for Quick-Fuse Appliqué. If you prefer traditional hand appliqué, be sure to reverse all appliqué templates and add ¼" seam allowance when cutting appliqué pieces. Refer to Hand Appliqué on page 109.

1. Refer to Quick-Fuse Appliqué instructions on page 109. Trace appliqué patterns on pages 37-39.

2. Referring to photo on page 32 and layout, position appliqués on blocks. Fuse appliqués in place and finish with machine satin stitch or decorative stitching as desired.

Assembly

1. Refer to photo on page 32 and layout. Arrange and sew blocks in two horizontal rows of three blocks each. Press seams in each row in opposite directions.

2. Sew rows together. Press.

Borders

1. Sew 1½" x 42" First Border strips end-to-end to make one continuous 1½"-wide strip. Refer to Adding the Borders on page 110. Measure quilt through center from side to side. Cut two 1½"-wide strips to that measurement. Sew to top and bottom of quilt. Press seams toward border.

2. Measure quilt through center from top to bottom, including borders just added. Cut two 1½"-wide First Border strips to that measurement. Sew to sides of quilt. Press.

3. <u>For directional fabric</u>, refer to Mitered Borders on page 110. Sew 72½" x 3½" Outside Border strips to top and bottom of quilt. Press seams toward borders. Sew 52½" x 3½" Outside Border strips to sides of quilt, mitering corners. Press seams toward borders.

<u>For non-directional fabric</u>, cut and sew six 3½" x 42" Outside Border strips end-to-end to make one continuous 3½"-wide strip. Refer to steps 1 and 2 to fit, trim, and sew 3½"-wide Outside Border strips to top, bottom, and sides of quilt. Press seams toward borders.

Layering and Finishing

1. Cut backing fabric in half crosswise. Sew pieces together to make one 80" x 55" (approximate) backing piece. Press. Arrange and baste backing, batting, and top together, referring to Layering the Quilt on page 111.

2. Hand or machine quilt as desired.

3. Sew 2¾" x 42" binding strips end-to-end to make one continuous 2¾"-wide strip. Refer to Binding the Quilt on page 111 and bind quilt to finish.

Forest Friends Wall Quilt
Finished Size: 69" x 49"
Photo: page 32

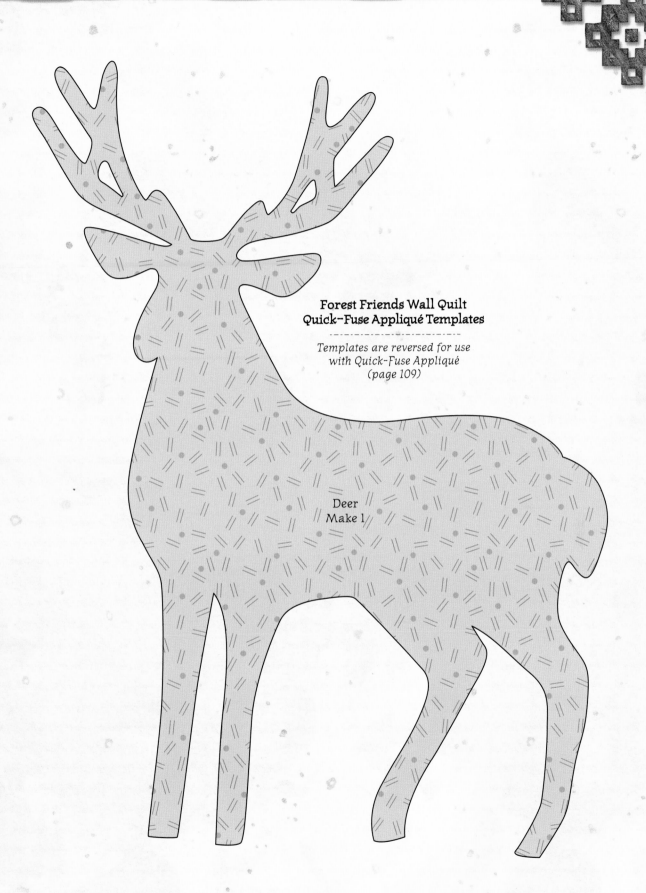

Forest Friends Wall Quilt
Quick-Fuse Appliqué Templates

Templates are reversed for use
with Quick-Fuse Appliqué
(page 109)

Deer
Make 1

Bear
Make 1 and 1 reversed

Wolf
Make 1

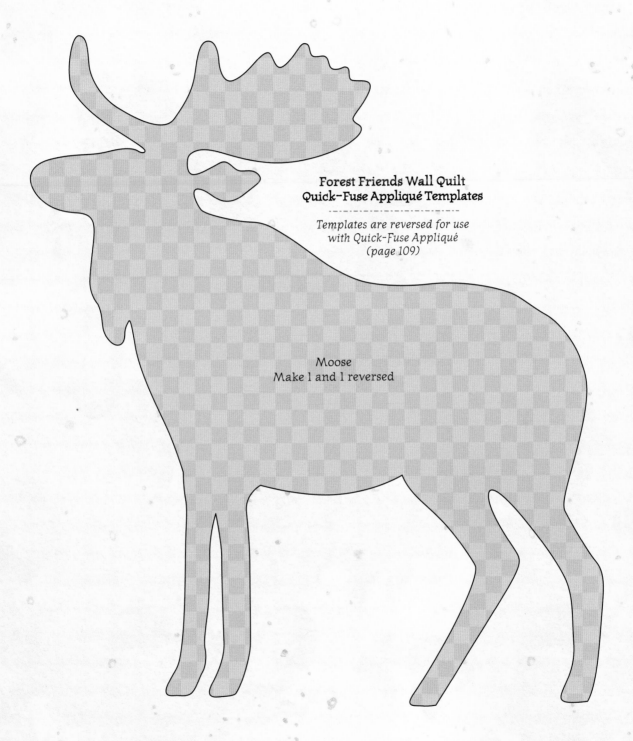

Forest Friends Wall Quilt
Quick-Fuse Appliqué Templates

*Templates are reversed for use
with Quick-Fuse Appliqué
(page 109)*

Moose
Make 1 and 1 reversed

Majestic Mountain Wall Quilt

Finished size: 27" x 49"

I can see Mount Spokane as I drive down the hill to work everyday. At this time of the year it is postcard-pretty with its cap of white snow and pine tree garland. Beautiful lakes surround us and a favorite holiday pastime is to go eagle watching at Lake Coeur d'Alene. The Pacific Northwest is well-known for its scenic beauty and the Majestic Mountain Wall Quilt captures this pristine grandeur in all its winter finery.

Fabric Requirements and Cutting Instructions

Read all instructions before beginning and use ¼"-wide seam allowances throughout. Read Cutting Strips and Pieces on page 108 prior to cutting fabrics.

Majestic Mountain Wall Quilt 27" x 49"	FIRST CUT Number of Strips or Pieces	FIRST CUT Dimensions	SECOND CUT Number of Pieces	SECOND CUT Dimensions
Fabric A Sky ½ yard	1	8½" x 42"	1	8½" x 20½"
			2	4½" squares
	1	2½" x 42"	2	2½" x 7½"
			2	2½" x 5½"
	3	1½" x 42"	2	1½" x 27½"
			1	1½" x 7½"
			1	1½" x 6½"
			1	1½" x 5½"
			1	1½" x 5"
			1	1½" x 3½"
			1	1½" x 3"
			1	1½" x 2½"
			8	1½" squares
Fabric B Mountain Snow ⅛ yard each of two fabrics	1	1½" x 42" _light snow_	1	1½" x 6½"
			1	1½" x 4½"
			1	1½" x 2½"
			4	1½" squares
	1	3½" x 42" _dark snow*_	1*	3½" x 1½"
			1*	3" x 1½"
Fabric C Mountain ⅛ yard	1	2½" x 42"	1	2½" x 14½"
			1	2½" x 6½"
			1	1½" x 4½"
			1	1½" x 3"
			1	1½" square
Fabric D Distant Mountain Scrap	2	2½" squares		
Fabric E Distant Foothills ⅛ yard	1	2½" x 42"	1	2½" x 7½"
			1	2½" x 4½"
			1	2½" x 3½"
			2	2½" squares
			1	1½" x 5½"
			1	1½" square
Fabric F Foothills ⅛ yard	1	2½" x 42"	1	2½" x 7½"
			1	1½" x 5½"
			1	1½" square
Fabric G Light Water ½ yard* (directional) OR ¼ yard (non-directional)	1	16½" x 42"	2*	16½" x 2½"
			1*	10½" x 2½"
			1*	9½" x 1½"
			1*	7½" x 3½"
			1	3½" square
			1	2½" square

*For directional fabric the measurement listed first runs parallel to selvage (strip width).

Majestic Mountain Wall Quilt Continued	FIRST CUT Number of Strips or Pieces	FIRST CUT Dimensions
Fabric H Dark Water ⅓ yard	1	3½" x 9½"
	1	3½" square
	2	2½" x 16½"
	1	2½" x 12½"
	1	2½" square
Fabric I Snow ¼ yard	1	4½" x 16½"
	1	1½" x 7½"
	1	1½" x 3½"
	1	1½" square
Shorelines _Assorted scraps_		
Shore A	1	3½" x 9½"
Shore B	1	2½" x 4½"
Shore C	1	2½" x 7½"
Shore D	1	1½" x 4½"
	1	1½" square
Shore E	1	2½" x 6½"

BORDERS

	FIRST CUT Number of Strips or Pieces	FIRST CUT Dimensions
Accent Border ⅙ yard	2	1½" x 27½"
	1	1½" x 6½"
First Border ⅙ yard	4	1" x 42"
Outside Border ¾ yard for bias		3" bias strips cut from 24" square
OR		OR
½ yard for straight cuts	4	3" x 42"
Binding ⅜ yard	4	2¾" x 42"

Lightweight Fusible Web - 1⅔ yards
Backing - 1½ yards
Batting - 32" x 54"
Pinecone, Pine Bough, Tree, and Snow Appliqués - Assorted scraps
Covered Buttons - kits for six ½" buttons and eight ⅜" buttons and assorted scraps

Assembling the Center Panel

Whenever possible, use the Assembly Line Method on page 108. Press in direction of arrows. Refer to Accurate Seam Allowance on page 108 prior to sewing.

1. Referring to Quick Corner Triangles on page 108, sew two 1½" Fabric A squares to 1½" x 4½" Fabric B piece as shown. Press. Sew unit between 1½" x 5½" and 1½" x 7½" Fabric A pieces as shown. Press.

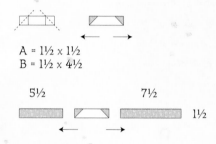

A = 1½ x 1½
B = 1½ x 4½

5½   7½   1½

2. Making a quick corner triangle unit, sew 1½" Fabric A square to 1½" x 6½" Fabric B piece as shown. Press. Sew 1½" x 3½" Fabric A piece to unit as shown. Press.

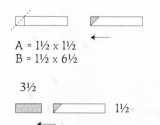

A = 1½ x 1½
B = 1½ x 6½

3½   1½

3. Making quick corner triangle units, sew 1½" Fabric A square and 1½" Fabric B square to 3" x 1½" Fabric B piece as shown. Press. Sew unit to 1½" x 5" Fabric A piece as shown. Press.

A = 1½ x 1½
B = 1½ x 1½
B = 3 x 1½

5

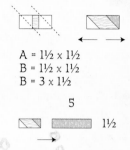   1½

4. Sew unit from step 2 to unit from step 3 as shown. Press.

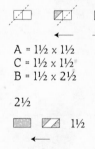

5. Making quick corner triangle units, sew 1½" Fabric A square and 1½" Fabric C square to 1½" x 2½" Fabric B piece as shown. Press. Sew unit to 1½" x 2½" Fabric A piece as shown. Press.

A = 1½ x 1½
C = 1½ x 1½
B = 1½ x 2½

2½

1½

6. Making a quick corner triangle unit, sew 1½" Fabric B square to 1½" x 4½" Fabric C piece as shown. Press. Making a quick corner triangle unit, sew 1½" Fabric B square to 1½" x 3" Fabric C piece as shown. Press. Sew units together as shown. Press.

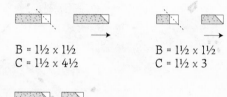

B = 1½ x 1½   B = 1½ x 1½
C = 1½ x 4½   C = 1½ x 3

7. Making quick corner triangle units, sew 1½" Fabric A square and 1½" Fabric B square to 3½" x 1½" Fabric B piece as shown. Press. Sew unit to 1½" x 3" Fabric A piece as shown. Press.

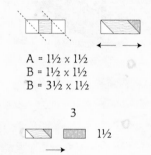

A = 1½ x 1½
B = 1½ x 1½
B = 3½ x 1½

3

1½

8. Sew unit from step 6 between units from steps 5 and 7 as shown. Press.

9. Making a quick corner triangle unit, sew 2½" Fabric D square to 2½" x 14½" Fabric C piece as shown. Press. Sew unit to 2½" Fabric D square as shown. Press.

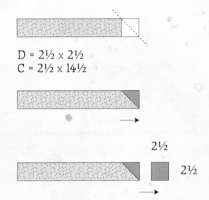

D = 2½ x 2½
C = 2½ x 14½

2½

2½

10. Making quick corner triangle units, sew two 2½" Fabric E squares to 2½" x 6½" Fabric C piece as shown. Press. Sew unit between 2½" x 3½" and 2½" x 7½" Fabric E pieces as shown. Press.

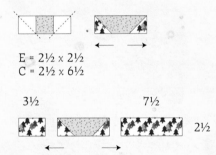

E = 2½ x 2½
C = 2½ x 6½

3½   7½

2½

11. Making a quick corner triangle unit, sew 1½" Fabric F square to 1½" x 5½" Fabric E piece as shown. Press. Making a quick corner triangle unit, sew 1½" Fabric E square to 1½" x 5½" Fabric F piece as shown. Press. Sew units together as shown. Press.

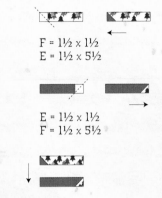

F = 1½ x 1½
E = 1½ x 5½

E = 1½ x 1½
F = 1½ x 5½

12. Sew unit from step 11 between 2½" x 7½" Fabric F piece and 2½" x 4½" Fabric E piece as shown. Press.

7½   4½

2½

13. Sew units from steps 1, 4, 8, 9, 10, 12, and 16½" x 2½" Fabric G strip together as shown. Press.

16½

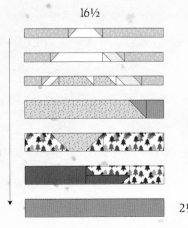

2½

There are 75 lakes within 50 miles of Spokane, so residents love going to their favorite lakeside retreats both summer and winter.

14. Making a quick corner triangle unit, sew 3½" Fabric G square to 3½" x 9½" Shore A piece as shown. Sew unit to 7½" x 3½" Fabric G piece as shown. Press.

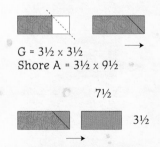

G = 3½ x 3½
Shore A = 3½ x 9½

7½

3½

15. Making a quick corner triangle unit, sew 2½" Fabric H square to 2½" x 4½" Shore B piece as shown. Press. Sew unit to 2½" x 12½" Fabric H piece as shown. Press.

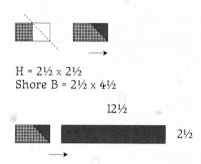

H = 2½ x 2½
Shore B = 2½ x 4½

12½

2½

17. Making a quick corner triangle unit, sew 3½" Fabric H square to unit from step 16 as shown. Press. Sew 3½" x 9½" Fabric H piece to unit as shown. Press.

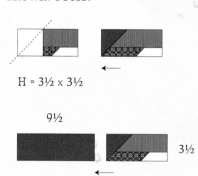

H = 3½ x 3½

9½

3½

18. Making a quick corner triangle unit, sew 2½" Fabric G square to 2½" x 6½" Shore E piece as shown. Press. Sew 10½" x 2½" Fabric G piece to unit as shown. Press.

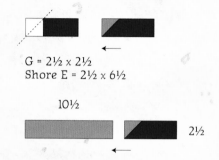

G = 2½ x 2½
Shore E = 2½ x 6½

10½

2½

16. Making a quick corner triangle unit, sew 1½" Shore D square to 1½" x 3½" Fabric I piece as shown. Press. Sew 1½" x 4½" Shore D piece to unit as shown. Press. Sew 2½" x 7½" Shore C piece to unit as shown. Press.

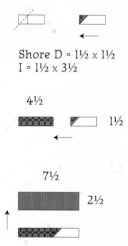

Shore D = 1½ x 1½
I = 1½ x 3½

4½

1½

7½

2½

19. To unit from step 13, sew unit from step 14, 2½" x 16½" Fabric H piece, unit from step 15, 16½" x 2½" Fabric G piece, unit from step 17, unit from step 18, and 2½" x 16½" Fabric H piece as shown. Press.

16½

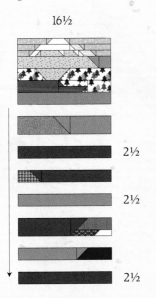

2½

2½

2½

20. Making a quick corner triangle unit, sew 1½" Fabric I square to 9½" x 1½" Fabric G piece as shown. Press. Sew 1½" x 7½" Fabric I piece to unit as shown. Press.

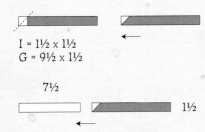

I = 1½ x 1½
G = 9½ x 1½

7½

1½

21. Making quick corner triangle units, sew two 4½" Fabric A squares to 4½" x 16½" Fabric I piece as shown. Press.

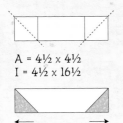

A = 4½ x 4½
I = 4½ x 16½

22. Making quick corner triangle units, sew two 1½" Fabric A squares to 1½" x 6½" Accent Border piece as shown. Press. Sew unit to 1½" x 6½" Fabric A piece as shown. Press.

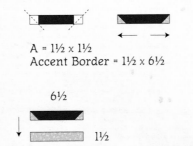

A = 1½ x 1½
Accent Border = 1½ x 6½

6½

1½

23. Sew unit from step 22 between two 2½" x 5½" Fabric A pieces as shown. Press.

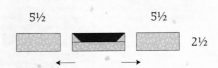

5½   5½

2½

24. Sew unit from step 21 between unit from step 20 and unit from step 23 as shown. Press.

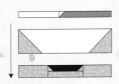

25. Sew unit from step 24 between two 2½" x 7½" Fabric A pieces as shown. Press.

2½   2½

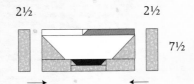

7½

26. Sew 1½" x 27½" Accent Border strip and 1½" x 27½" Fabric A piece together. Press toward Accent Border. Make two. Sew units to sides of center panel. Press. Sew center panel between 8½" x 20½" Fabric A piece and unit from step 25 as shown. Press. Center panel measures 20½" x 42½".

20½

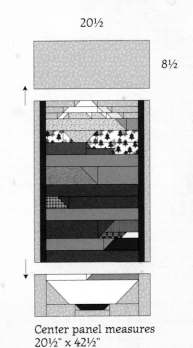

8½

Center panel measures
20½" x 42½"

Adding the Appliqués

The instructions given are for Quick-Fuse Appliqué. If you prefer traditional hand appliqué, be sure to reverse all appliqué templates and add ¼"-wide seam allowances when cutting appliqué pieces. Refer to Hand Appliqué directions on page 109.

1. Referring to Quick-Fuse Appliqué and Appliqué Pressing Sheet on page 109, trace appliqué templates on pages 47-49 for trees, snow, large pinecone, and tree trunk. Refer to page 67 for small pinecone. For boughs, make three of Pine Bough A and three reversed, one of Pine Bough B and one reversed, one of Pine Bough C and one reversed. Cut snow-covered boughs using Pine Bough C making four and four reversed.

2. Referring to photo on page 40 and layout, position appliqués on center panel. Fuse appliqués in place and finish with machine satin stitch or decorative stitching as desired.

Borders

1. Sew 1½"-wide First Border strips end-to-end to make one continuous 1½"-wide strip. Measure quilt through center from side to side. Trim two 1½"-wide First Border strips to that measurement. Sew to top and bottom of quilt. Press toward border.

2. Measure quilt through center from top to bottom including borders just added. Cut two 1½"-wide First Border strips to that measurement. Sew to sides of quilt. Press.

3. Referring to Making Bias Strips on page 110, sew 3"-wide bias strips end-to-end to make one continuous strip. Approximately 170" of bias strip is needed. Repeat steps 1 and 2 to fit, trim, and sew 3"-wide Outside Border strips to quilt.

Layering and Finishing

1. Trim backing to make one 32" x 54" (approximate) backing piece. Arrange and baste backing, batting, and top together, referring to Layering the Quilt on page 111.

2. Hand or machine quilt as desired.

3. Sew 2¾" x 42" binding strips end-to-end to make one continuous 2¾"-wide strip. Refer to Binding the Quilt on page 111 and bind quilt to finish.

4. Cover fourteen buttons with red fabric following manufacturer's instructions. Referring to photo on page 40 and layout for placement, sew buttons to quilt.

Majestic Mountain Wall Quilt
Finished Size: 27" x 49"
Photo: page 40

Tracing Line _____
Embroidery Line ·················

Pine Bough C

Berry for
Holiday Pines
Tree Skirt

Pine Bough and Pinecone
Appliqué Templates

Pine Bough A

Pinecone

Pine Bough B

Make 1

Make 3 and 3 reversed

Make 2

Make 3

Make 3

Make 1

Make 1 and 1 reversed

Make 1

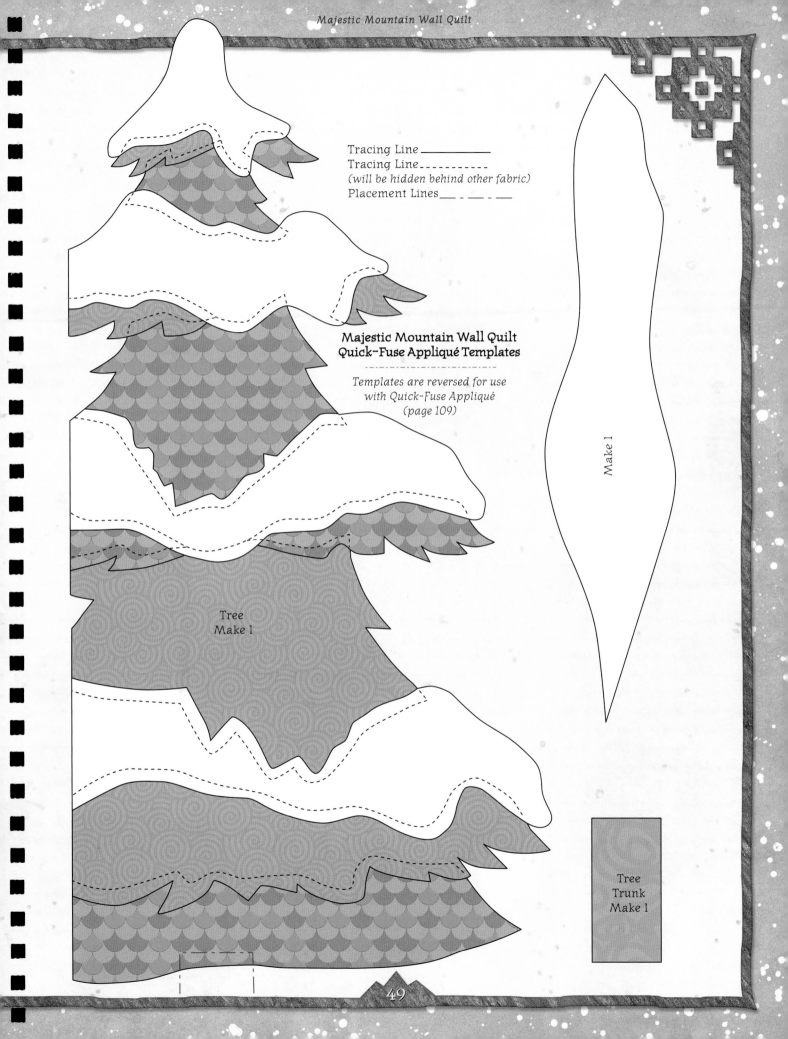

Tracing Line _____
Tracing Line - - - - - - - - -
(will be hidden behind other fabric)
Placement Lines __ _ __ _ __

Majestic Mountain Wall Quilt
Quick-Fuse Appliqué Templates

Templates are reversed for use
with Quick-Fuse Appliqué
(page 109)

Make 1

Tree
Make 1

Tree
Trunk
Make 1

North Country Stockings

Finished size: 19" long

Remember the excitement of Christmas
morning when you were a child? The brightly lit tree, the piles of presents, the bulging stockings?
There's something about Christmas that returns all of us to that magical time in
our youth. I love everything about the holidays and a gift-filled stocking
is still one of my favorite things! Our North Country Stockings are fun and fanciful—
even when they're not filled with presents!

Making the North Country Stocking Pattern

Trace Stocking Pattern, Part 1 and 2 from pages 54-55, matching markings. Extend top of Stocking Pattern by attaching an 8½" x 11" paper at star markings. Align straight edges and mark paper as shown. Cut out Stocking Pattern.

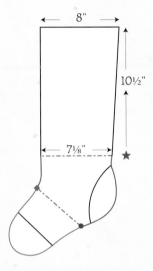

Fabric Requirements and Cutting Instructions

Read all instructions before beginning and use ¼"-wide seam allowances throughout. Read Cutting Strips and Pieces on page 108 prior to cutting fabrics.

Forest Friends Stocking

Forest Friends Stocking 19" Long	FIRST CUT	
	Number of Strips or Pieces	Dimensions
Stocking ⅝ yard for bias cut OR ⅓ yard for straight cut		Place pattern on the diagonal and cut.
Cuff ⅓ yard	1	8½" x 16"
Silhouette Background Scrap	1	4½" square
	1	4" x 3"

Bear, Moose and Toe Appliqués - Scraps
Lining - ⅓ yard
Batting - 28" x 28"
Leather Lacing - 6"
Fusible Web - ⅛ yard
Embroidery Floss

Making the Forest Friends Stocking

1. Place stocking fabric on batting. Quilt as desired. Trace stocking pattern onto quilted piece. Cut out one stocking and one reversed for back.

2. Referring to Quick-Fuse Appliqué on page 109 and toe pattern on page 55, position and fuse toe piece to stocking front. Machine or hand stitch straight edge of toe to stocking front with decorative stitching as desired.

3. Referring to Quick-Fuse Appliqué on page 109 and appliqué templates on pages 53 and 55, position and fuse Moose appliqué on 4½" Silhouette Background square and Bear on 4" x 3" Silhouette Background piece.

4. Referring to photo, position and fuse Silhouette Background pieces to stocking front. Referring to Embroidery Stitch Guide on page 108, stitch background pieces to stocking front with elongated overcast stitching or as desired.

5. Place stocking front and back right sides together. Stitch along sides of stocking, leaving top edge free. Turn right side out.

6. Fold lining fabric right sides together, pin, and cut using Stocking Pattern. Stitch along sides of lining, leaving top edge free.

7. With right sides together, sew short ends of 8½" x 16" Cuff piece together. Press seam open. Fold cuff in half with wrong sides together.

8. Place stocking lining unit from step 6 inside stocking with wrong sides together. Place ends of 6" loop of leather lacing at back edge of lining for hanging. Stay stitch ⅛" from outside edge. Place folded cuff inside lining, aligning raw edges and stitch cuff to stocking and lining. Turn cuff to right side of stocking.

Cozy Lodge Stocking

Cozy Lodge Stocking 19" Long	FIRST CUT	
	Number of Strips or Pieces	Dimensions
Stocking *Assorted Scraps**	81* 63*	2" x 3½" 1½" x 3½"
Cuff ¼ yard	1	9½" x 16"

Lining - ⅓ yard
Batting - 28" x 28"
¼"-wide Ribbon - ⅔ yard
Leather Lacing - 6"
1" Bells - 2
*We used leftover Bargello segments from page 28 to make our stocking. If using different fabrics, cut pieces indicated.

Making the Cozy Lodge Stocking

1. Leftover Bargello segments from the Cozy Lodge Quilt on page 28 can be used for this project. If not using leftover Bargello units, refer to photo and Cutting Chart, to arrange and sew together eighty-one 2" x 3½" pieces in nine rows of nine pieces each and sixty-three 1½" x 3½" pieces in seven rows of nine pieces each. Press.

2. Save time by sewing strips and quilting at the same time. Referring to photo for placement, lay two strips right sides together on batting. Stitch ¼"-wide seam through strips and batting. Press. Repeat process to sew additional strips.

3. Trace Stocking Pattern (page 51) onto quilted piece. Cut out one stocking and one reversed for back.

4. Refer to Forest Friends Stocking, steps 6 thru 8, and substitute 9½" x 16" Cuff piece. Quilt animal silhouette on cuff if desired. Sew stocking together. Complete next step before turning cuff.

5. Measure ¾" from folded edge of cuff and stay-stitch (10-12 stitches per inch) around the entire cuff. Using scissors, cut fold open, then cut ¼"-wide fringe to stay-stitching. Turn cuff to right side of stocking.

6. Tie bells to ends of ribbon. Refer to photo to wrap ribbon around cuff and tack in place at sides of cuff. Loosely tie ribbon in front.

Woodland Charm Stocking

Woodland Charm Stocking 19" Long	FIRST CUT	
	Number of Strips or Pieces	Dimensions
Stocking ⅝ yard (directional) OR ⅓ yard (non-directional)		
Cuff ½ yard (directional) OR ⅛ yard (non-directional)	1	16" x 3½"
Cuff Trim ¼ yard	1	6" x 16"

Heel and Toe Appliqués - Scraps
Lining - ⅓ yard
Batting - 28" x 28"
Lightweight Fusible Web - Scrap
Rickrack - 1 yard
Leather Lacing - 6"
Assorted Wood Ornaments
1½" Simulated Bone Beads - 5
½" Bells - 5
Sandpaper
Antiquing Medium
Red Perle Cotton
Acrylic Paints - Red, black, and gold
Matte Spray Varnish
Paintbrush

Making the Woodland Charm Stocking

1. Place stocking fabric on batting. Quilt as desired. Trace Stocking Pattern (page 51) onto quilted piece, cut one and one reversed for back.

2. Trace toe and heel Patterns from pages 54-55. Referring to Quick-Fuse Appliqué on page 109, position and fuse toe and heel pieces to stocking front. Stitch rickrack trim over straight edge of toe piece and inside curved edge of heel piece.

3. With right sides together, sew one long edge of 16" x 3½" Cuff piece and one long edge of 6" x 16" Cuff Trim piece together. Press.

4. With right sides together, sew short ends of cuff together. Press seam open. Fold cuff in half with wrong sides together. Refer to photo to stitch rickrack trim on right side of cuff.

5. Referring to Forest Friends Stocking steps 6 thru 8, substituting pieced cuff from step 4, and placing rickrack side to right side of lining, sew stocking, lining, and cuff together.

6. Using a paintbrush, apply acrylic paint to purchased wood ornaments. Paint the bear black, the bird red, and the stars gold. Allow to dry. Sand ornament edges. Apply antiquing according to manu-facturer's directions. When dry, spray ornaments with matte varnish. Referring to photo, use perle cotton to attach ornaments, beads, and bells to cuff.

Bears and moose, deer and wolves will take up residence in your personal pine forest this Christmas. Quick-fuse appliqué makes these ornaments a fast and easy addition to your tree.

Make three different ornament designs with just a few changes.

Materials Needed
Silhouette Background - Assorted scraps
  One 6" square
  Two 3¾" squares
Border - Assorted scraps
  Two 6" squares
Backing - Assorted scraps
  Three 6" squares
Forest Friends Appliqué - Assorted scraps
Leather Lacing
Heavyweight Fusible Web - Scraps
Embroidery Floss - Tan, green, red

Moose or Deer Ornament

1. *Referring to Quick-Fuse Appliqué on page 109, trace deer or moose templates on pages 54-55. Cut and fuse appliqué to 6" Silhouette Background fabric.*

2. *Position unit from step 1 and 6" Backing square, right sides together. Center both pieces on top of batting and pin all three layers together. Using a ¼"-wide seam allowance, sew around all edges, leaving a 3" opening for turning. Trim batting close to stitching. Clip corners, turn, and press. Hand stitch opening closed.*

3. *Referring to Embroidery Stitch Guide on page 108, use an elongated overcast stitch to stitch along outside edge with six strands of embroidery floss. Attach leather lacing for hanger.*

Wolf and Bear Ornaments

1. *Refer to photos and to Quick-Fuse Appliqué on page 109. Fuse 3¾" Background square to 6" Border square. Background squares can be arranged in two different ways. Trace and fuse wolf (page 55) or bear to unit. Make two, one of each variation.*

2. *Refer to steps 2 and 3 to complete ornaments.*

Bear Ornament Template

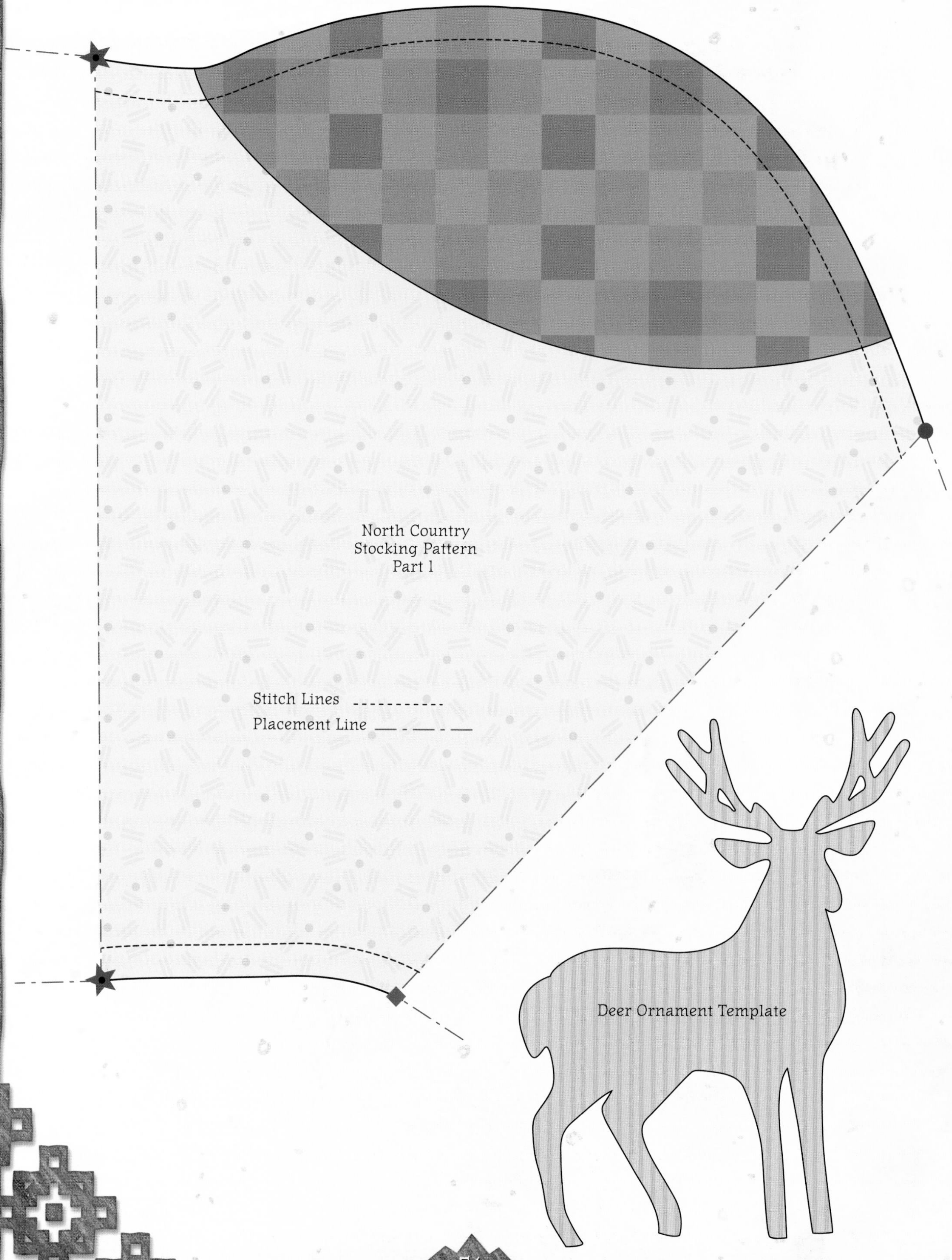

North Country
Stocking Pattern
Part 1

Stitch Lines ----------
Placement Line — — · — · —

Deer Ornament Template

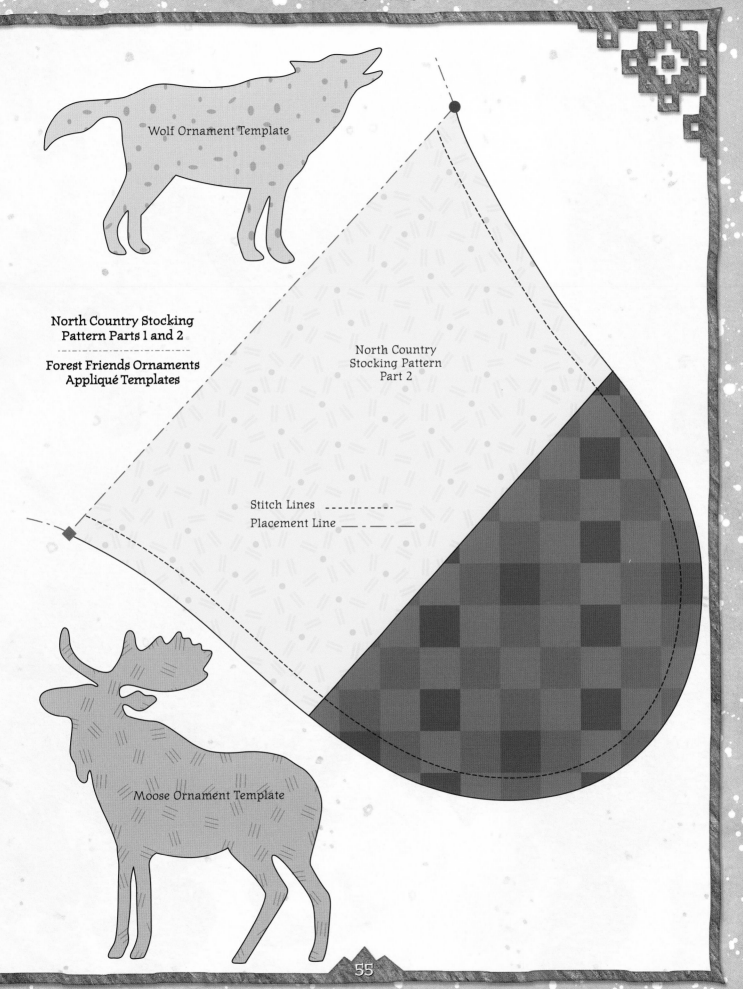

Wolf Ornament Template

**North Country Stocking
Pattern Parts 1 and 2**

**Forest Friends Ornaments
Appliqué Templates**

North Country
Stocking Pattern
Part 2

Stitch Lines   – – – – – – –
Placement Line   — · — · — · —

Moose Ornament Template

Pinecone Trees in Woodland Pots

When I walk through the woods in summer and fall, I fill my pockets with small pinecones, nuts, and other small gifts of nature. I love the textures and colors of these woodland surprises. Now, with snow on the ground, I have time to use my natural collection to make pinecone trees to decorate the holiday hearth. Terra cotta pots painted in woodsy plaids and checks are the perfect containers for these pinecone trees.

Materials Needed

8" and 10" Terra cotta flowerpots
Gesso
Acrylic paints in ivory,
   light tan, medium green,
   dark green, red, black
Assorted paintbrushes
Sea sponge
Miracle Sponge™*
Crackle medium
Ruler
Pencil
Craft scissors
Matte spray varnish
Sandpaper *(fine grit)*

* Miracle Sponge is thinly compressed cellulose that expands when wet. It is available at many art and craft supply stores.

Paint clean, dry flowerpots inside and out with gesso to prepare surfaces for painting.
   Note: allow paint to dry thoroughly between each step.

Painting the Plaid Pot

1. Basecoat 8" flowerpot with ivory paint.

2. Dampen a sea sponge and wring well. Dip sea sponge in light tan paint then ivory paint and blot on a paper towel. Using a tapping motion, sponge tan/ivory paint over the entire flowerpot. Use a light touch for a mottled effect. Sponge more tan paint on the flowerpot rim, applying heavily at the top edge for a darker effect.

3. Using ruler and pencil, evenly mark vertical stripes for plaid. Because flowerpots are conical, marking lines should be approximately 1½" apart at the base and 2" apart just under the rim.

4. Using a 1"-wide paintbrush, paint vertical red stripes on lines just drawn. Center the stripe over the drawn line.

5. Repeat marking and painting for horizontal red stripes spacing evenly.

6. Mix red paint with black and darken squares where the stripes overlap.

7. Using green paint and a smaller paintbrush, paint narrow vertical and horizontal stripes near the red stripes. Refer to photo for details.

8. Use black paint and a small brush to add vertical and horizontal stripes in the center of the red plaid. When dry, lightly sand the painted stripes to age and add texture to the plaid.

9. Using a pencil and ruler, mark a 1" square on Miracle Sponge™ and cut with craft scissors. Dampen Miracle Sponge™ to expand, then wring well. Square will be about ⅛" larger when expanded.

10. Dip sponge in medium green then dark green paint, blot on a paper towel and use sponge to stamp diamond shapes along the rim of pot.

11. Paint a red stripe on top edge of rim and finish inside of pot with red paint.

12. When completely dry, spray with several coats of matte varnish following manufacturer's directions.
   Note: If using pot to hold a plant rather than pinecone tree, do not plant directly in the painted pot as moisture from watering can damage the painted finish.

3. Dampen and wring sea sponge. Dip in a rough mix of red and black paint and sponge on the rim to achieve a mottled finish.

4. Using pencil and ruler, draw 1⅜", 1⅛", and 1" squares on Miracle Sponge™ and cut out. Dampen Miracle Sponge™ squares in water to expand, then wring thoroughly. Squares will be about ⅛" larger when sponge is expanded.

Painting the Checked Pot

1. Basecoat rim of 10" pot with red paint; basecoat the rest of the pot with black paint.

2. When dry, following manufacturer's directions, apply crackle medium to black portion of the pot and allow to "set" as directed. Apply a quick even coat of a rough mix of the two green paint colors to the same area. Crackles will appear in the painted surface. Do not touch, as the surface is very fragile when wet. Allow to dry thoroughly.

5. Dip largest sponge square in black paint, blot on paper towel and stamp first row of checks on the pot starting just below the rim. Stamp one square then skip an equal amount of space before stamping the next square to form a checkerboard pattern. After stamping the first row with the largest sponge, do two rows using the 1⅛" sponge, and three rows using the 1" sponge. Stamp squares farther apart on top rows and closer together for lower rows to compensate for the conical shape of the pot.

6. When completely dry, spray with several coats of matte varnish, following manufacturer's directions.

The Northwest is well known for its fantastic skiing. From graceful skiers like our friend, Jay, to the playful and daring snowboarders like my son, Murphy, everyone has fun on the slopes.

Mantel Miniatures

Materials Needed to Make the Pinecone Trees

Assorted dried pinecones, pods, nuts, and other natural elements

Round Styrofoam topiary form (*available at craft stores*)

Twig or Styrofoam tree-shaped base

Glue gun and sticks

¾" to 1" branch for tree trunk

Matte spray varnish

Plaster of Paris

Moss

Twigs

Raffia

Making the Pinecone Trees *(Photo page 56)*

1. Apply hot glue to base of each pinecone and glue to topiary form. Place pinecones and natural elements as close together as possible to fill all spaces on the form. For variety, use a mixture of sizes and shapes. Fill small spaces between cones with moss. When forms are completely covered and you are satisfied with your arrangement, spray cone trees with matte varnish to help preserve your project.

2. For the tree-shape, glue pinecones from the bottom up, being careful to finish with a nice cone on top of the tree. Insert a branch into the tree base to serve as the tree trunk. Mix Plaster of Paris according to package directions and pour into painted pot, insert tree trunk in wet plaster, and hold in place until plaster is dry. Place a layer of moss on top of plaster to finish.

3. For the round topiary, wrap small twigs around the trunk of the topiary and use hot glue to affix. Insert topiary form into painted pot and weight with sand or Plaster of Paris, if needed. Finish with a layer of moss and embellish with a raffia bow.

Create a small forest on your mantel by using individual cones as topiaries!

Paint a variety of small pots using techniques described on pages 57–58. Select large, nicely shaped pinecones to serve as "trees."

Line painted pots with fresh or faux greenery to provide a base for pinecones. Set pinecones on top. If desired, add berries to the arrangement.

Painted pots can also be filled with twigs dusted with glitter or a small arrangement of pinecones and natural elements. Finish the mantel with fresh greenery, berries, apples, and additional pinecones.

The fireplace brings welcome warmth and candlelight adds sparkle in the deepening twilight. Fresh greenery brings the outdoors inside and the tree is decked with nature's bounty. The beauty of the woodlands is celebrated in colorful quilts as the family gathers at the table for merriment and good cheer.

Woodland Botanicals

Woodland Beauty Lap Quilt

Finished size: 64" x 64"

I love living in a place where blue jeans are the preferred mode of dress, where everyone feels an intimate connection with nature, and where the great outdoors ARE just outside the door. This quilt captures that feeling. With its denim blocks, wool appliqués featuring beautiful botanicals and birds, and its pieced blocks in earthy colors, it typifies the natural abundance and beauty of the Northwest.

Fabric Requirements and Cutting Instructions

Read all instructions before beginning and use ¼"-wide seam allowances throughout. Read Cutting Strips and Pieces on page 108 prior to cutting fabrics.

Woodland Beauty Lap Quilt 64" x 64"	FIRST CUT		SECOND CUT	
	Number of Strips or Pieces	Dimensions	Number of Pieces	Dimensions
Fabric A (Denim) Block A Background 1⅝ yards OR ⅞ yard of 60"-wide fabric	8	14" squares		
Fabric B Block B Centers *Assorted scraps*	32	6½" squares		
Fabric C Block B Corners ⅙ yard each of eight fabrics	1*	4½" x 42" *Cut for each of eight fabrics*	4*	4½" squares
Fabric D First Border and Corner Block ⅞ yard	5 3	4" x 42" 1¾" x 42"	8 8	1¾" x 8" 1¾" x 5½"
Fabric E Sawtooth Border Triangles ½ yard	3	5" x 42"	24	5" squares
Fabric F (Denim) Sawtooth Border Triangles ½ yard	3	5" x 42"	24	5" squares
Fabric G Corner Block Centers ⅛ yard	4	3½" squares		
Fabric H Corner Block Accent ⅙ yard	2	1½" x 42"	8 8	1½" x 5½" 1½" x 3½"
Binding ⅝ yard	7	2¾" x 42"		

Leaf and Pine Bough Appliqués - ⅙ yard each of seven fabrics**
Bird, Pinecone, Berry, and Branch Appliqués - Assorted scraps**
Backing - 4 yards
Batting - 70" x 70"
Stabilizer - 2 yards
Embroidery Thread or Floss and Perle Cotton
Glue Stick

**We used felted or boiled wool*

The Woodland Beauty Lap Quilt features appliquéd denim blocks alternating with pieced blocks. Machine embroidery highlights both types of blocks. A sawtooth border and embroidery-accented corner squares add even more detail to this beautiful quilt.

Making the Blocks

You will be making eight of Block A and eight of Block B. Both Blocks A and B are embellished with decorative machine stitching using machine embroidery thread. The wool appliqués are attached with a triple, zigzag, or blanket stitch. It is recommended that you anchor beginning and ending stitches. If you prefer hand embroidery, refer to Embroidery Stitch Guide on page 108. All blocks measure 12½" square unfinished. Whenever possible, use the Assembly Line Method on page 108. Press seams in direction of arrows.

Block A

1. Using quilter's chalk or removable fabric marker, center and mark a 9½" square on right side of 14" Fabric A square. Place Fabric A square on top of stabilizer. Use sewing machine to stitch decorative stitches on marked lines. This embroidery stitching will create a frame for appliqué blocks. Make eight.

2. Refer to Woodland Beauty Appliqué Templates on pages 67-69 for bird, branches, leaves, cone, and berries; and page 47 for pine boughs, pine burs, pinecone, and branch appliqués. Refer to photo on page 62 and layout on page 66 to trace the number of appliqués desired.

3. Referring to pages 47 and 67 for pine bur placement, use a washable glue stick to position pine burs. Use a zigzag stitch to attach burs to pinecones or refer to Embroidery Stitch Guide on page 108 to use a satin stitch in place of pine bur appliqués.

4. Referring to photo on page 62 and layout on page 66, position and pin appliqués inside decorative stitching on Fabric A squares as desired. Use a zigzag stitch to attach branches to block. Use a triple stitch ⅛" from outside edge to attach pinecones. Anchor beginning and ending stitches. Use a triple stitch to attach leaves and boughs, sewing along vein lines and stems.

5. Referring to Berry Template on page 68, use perle cotton and straight stitches to attach berries with a pound sign (#) design.

6. Use a machine blanket stitch to attach bird. Referring to Embroidery Stitch Guide on page 108, stitch an eye using perle cotton and a French knot.

7. Square Block A to 12½". Make eight.

Block B

1. Referring to photo on page 62, sew together two 6½" Fabric B squares using assorted colors. Press. Make sixteen.

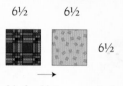

Make 16 in assorted colors

2. Sew together two units from step 1 as shown. Press. Make eight.

Make 8 in assorted colors

3. Referring to Quick Corner Triangles on page 108, sew four 4½" Fabric C squares to units from step 2 as shown. Press. Make eight. Blocks measure 12½".

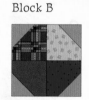

C = 4½ x 4½

Block B

Make 8 in assorted colors

Block measures 12½" square

4. Embellish seams with decorative stitching as desired.

TIPS FOR APPLIQUÉING WITH WOOL

Use felt or felted wool for appliqués. There is no need to add seam allowances or to turn under edges for felted wool. To felt your own wool, follow these steps:

1. Plunge the wool fabric in boiling water for 5 minutes, then plunge it into icy water until very chilled. Do not mix colors as dyes may run.

2. Blot the wool with a dry towel and place both towel and wool in dryer on high heat until thoroughly dry. The result is a thicker, fuller fabric that will give added texture to the wool. Pressing felted wool is not recommended, as it will flatten the texture. Remember, most wools will shrink 10-15% when boiled.

Assembly

1. Refer to Accurate Seam Allowance page 108 prior to sewing. Referring to photo on page 62 and layout on page 66, arrange and sew Blocks A and B in four rows of four blocks each. Press seams in opposite directions from row to row. Sew rows together and press. Top measures 48½" square.

2. Sew 4" x 42" Fabric D strips end-to-end to make one continuous 4"-wide strip. Press. Cut four 4" x 48½" sections.

3. Draw a diagonal line on wrong side of 5" Fabric E square. Place Fabric E square on top of 5" Fabric F square with right sides together. Sew a scant ¼" away from both sides of drawn line to make half-square triangles. Make twenty-four. Cut on drawn line and press toward Fabric E. Make forty-eight. Square to 4½".

E = 5 x 5
F = 5 x 5
Make 24

Make 48
Square to 4½"

4. Sew together twelve units from step 3 as shown. Press. Sew 4" x 48½" Fabric D section from step 2 to unit as shown to make border unit. Press. Make four.

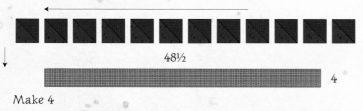

48½

4

Make 4

5. Referring to photo on page 62 and layout on page 66, sew two units from step 4 to top and bottom of quilt. Press seams toward border.

---

6. Sew 3½" Fabric G square between two 1½" x 3½" Fabric H pieces as shown. Press. Make four.

3½

1½

3½

1½

Make 4

7. Sew unit from step 6 between two 1½" x 5½" Fabric H pieces as shown. Press. Make four.

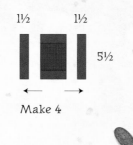

1½   1½

5½

Make 4

Woodland Patchwork Ornaments

Celebrate the colors of nature while using leftovers from other projects with these pretty patchwork ornaments. Machine embroidery highlights the patches.

Materials for One Ornament:
Fabric A Block Center - Assorted scraps
  Four 2½" squares
Fabric B Block Corners - Scrap
  Four 1¾" squares
Backing - One 4½" square
Polyester fiberfill
Perle cotton

1. *Refer to Woodland Beauty Lap Quilt Block B page 64, steps 1-3 for diagrams, substituting Fabrics B and C with Fabrics A and B above. Make two in step 1 and one in steps 2 and 3. Block measures 4½". Embellish seams with decorative stitching as desired.*

2. *Place block and backing right sides together. Sew around edges, leaving a 2" opening for turning and stuffing. Clip corners, turn right side out, and press. Stuff lightly and hand stitch opening closed.*

3. *Make a hanging loop with 6" piece of perle cotton. Embellish with assorted buttons, if desired.*

8. Sew unit from step 7 between two 1¾" x 5½" Fabric D pieces as shown. Press. Make four.

5½

1¾

1¾

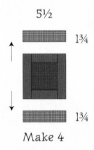

Make 4

9. Sew unit from step 8 between two 1¾" x 8" Fabric D pieces as shown. Press. Make four. Corner Block measures 8" square. Embellish with decorative stitches as desired.

1¾   1¾

8

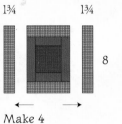

Make 4
Block measures 8" square

10. Referring to photo on page 62 and layout, sew border unit from step 4 between two units from step 9. Press. Make two. Sew to sides of quilt. Press.

There's nothing more beautiful than snow-frosted trees in the sparkling light of winter sunshine! You don't have to go far in the Northwest to find this pristine beauty.

Woodland Beauty Lap Quilt
Finished Size: 64" x 64"
Photo: page 62

Layering and Finishing

1. Cut backing crosswise into two equal pieces. Sew pieces together to make one 83" x 70" (approximate) backing piece. Press. Cut backing to 70" x 70". Arrange and baste backing, batting, and top together, referring to Layering the Quilt on page 111.

2. Hand or machine quilt as desired.

3. Sew 2¾" x 42" binding strips end-to-end to make one continuous 2¾"-wide strip. Refer to Binding the Quilt on page 111 and bind quilt to finish.

Woodland Beauty Lap Quilt
Appliqué Template

Tracing Line _____
Tracing Line - - - - - - - - - - -
(will be hidden behind other fabric)
Embroidery Lines ....

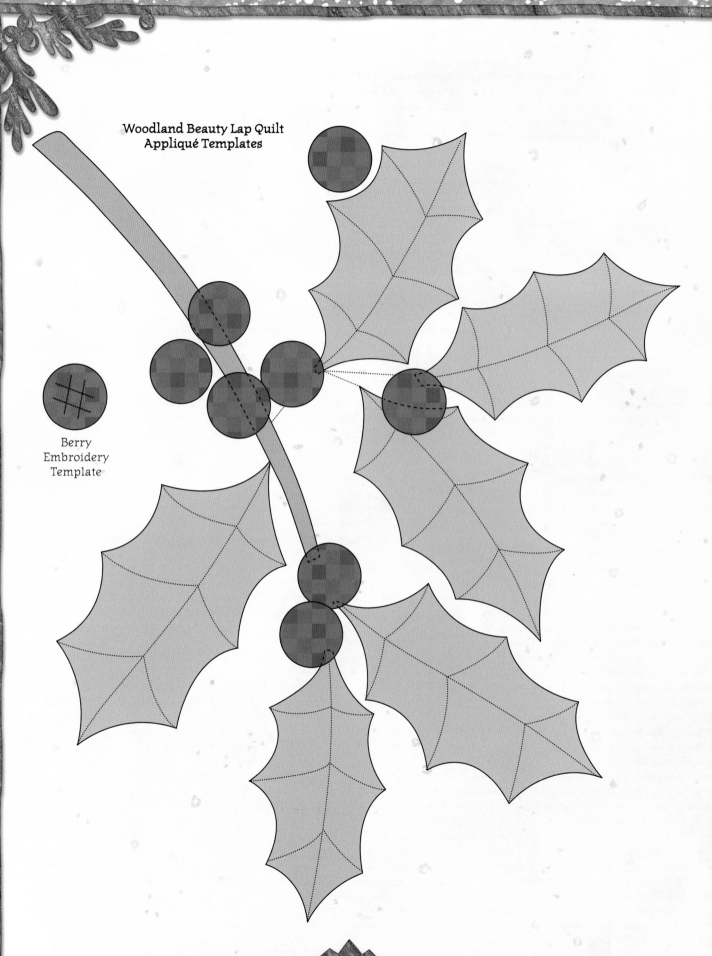

Woodland Beauty Lap Quilt
Appliqué Templates

Berry
Embroidery
Template

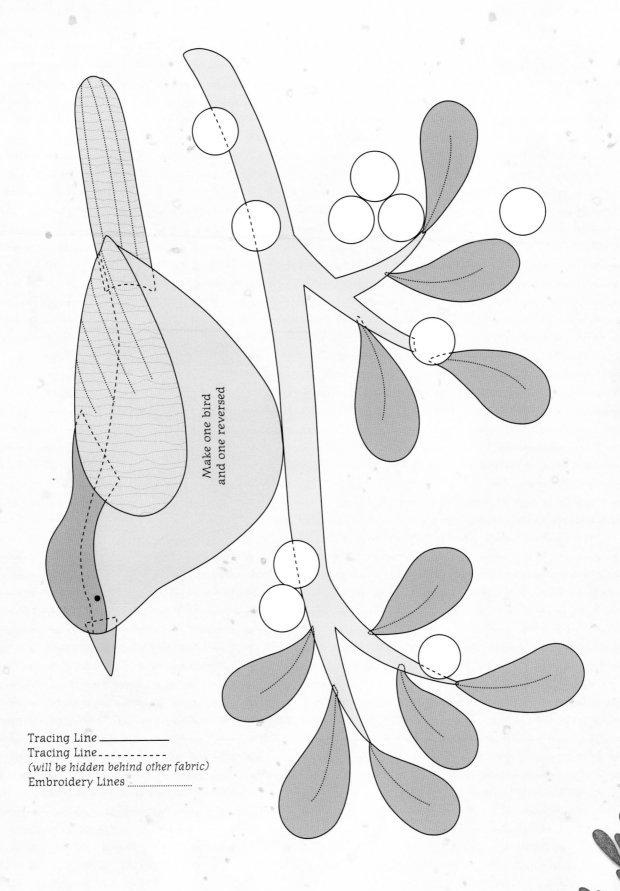

Make one bird
and one reversed

Tracing Line _____
Tracing Line - - - - - - - - - - -
(will be hidden behind other fabric)
Embroidery Lines ....

Berries and Vines
Table Runner and Placemats

Finished size: 48" x 14"

One thing the Northwest is famous for is our love of coffee and good food! Espresso stands are on every corner and our favorite brews are part of our daily lives. Many cuisines are enjoyed, and seafood is a natural favorite. To welcome dinner guests and please the eye, this table runner and placemats are the perfect partners. Embroidered berries and Big Stitch vines bring botanical beauty to the table.

Fabric Requirements and Cutting Instructions

Read all instructions before beginning and use ¼"-wide seam allowances throughout. Read Cutting Strips and Pieces on page 108 prior to cutting fabrics.

Berries and Vines Table Runner 48" x 14"	FIRST CUT		SECOND CUT	
	Number of Strips or Pieces	Dimensions	Number of Pieces	Dimensions
Fabric A Block Centers *Assorted scraps*	12	5½" squares		
Fabric B Block Corners *⅛ yard for each of three fabrics*	4*	3½" squares **cut for each fabric*		
Fabric C Side Setting Triangles *½ yard*	1	15½" x 42"	1	15½" square (cut twice diagonally)
Fabric D Corner Setting Triangles *⅓ yard*	1	8" x 42"	2	8" squares (cut once diagonally)
Fabric E Border *⅙ yard*	1	3½" x 42"	2	3½" x 14½"

Backing - ¾ yard
Batting - 52" x 18"
Embroidery Thread or Floss and Perle Cotton

Making the Table Runner

You will be making three blocks. Whenever possible, use the Assembly Line Method on page 108. Press seams in direction of arrows. Refer to Accurate Seam Allowance on page 108 prior to sewing. After quilting, embellish the runner with Big Stitch Quilting and decorative stitches.

1. Sew together two 5½" Fabric A squares. Press. Make six.

5½   5½
5½

Make 6 in assorted colors

2. Sew together two units from step 1 as shown. Press. Make three.

Make 3 in assorted colors

3. Refer to Quick Corner Triangles on page 108. Sew four 3½" Fabric B squares to unit from step 2 as shown. Press. Make three. Block measures 10½" square.

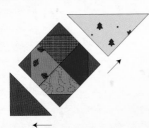

B = 3½ x 3½

Make 3
Block measures 10½" square

4. Sew block from step 3 between one Fabric C and one Fabric D triangle as shown. Press. Sew Fabric D triangle to side as shown. Press. Make two.

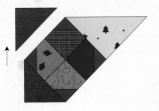

Make 2

Make 2

5. Sew remaining block from step 3 between two Fabric C triangles as shown. Press.

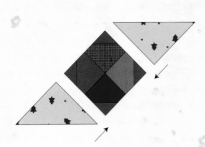

6. Sew unit from step 5 between units from step 4 as shown. Press. Sew unit between two 3½" x 14½" Fabric E pieces as shown. Press.

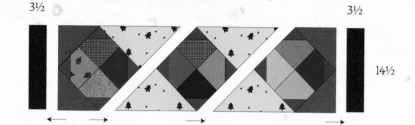

7. Trace Berries and Vine Embroidery Template, marking placement lines. Refer to photo on page 70, layout, and Embroidery Stitch Guide on page 108. Use three strands of embroidery floss and a satin stitch to stitch berries. Leaves and Vines will be stitched later as part of the quilting.

Layering and Finishing

1. Cut backing lengthwise into two equal pieces. Sew pieces together to make one 52" x 18" (approximate) backing piece. Press.

2. Layer top and backing, right sides together, on batting. Using a ¼"-wide seam, sew around edges leaving a 6" opening for turning. Trim batting close to stitching. Trim backing ¼" from seam line. Clip corners and turn. Press. Hand stitch opening closed.

3. Baste, then quilt as desired. Refer to Big Stitch Quilting on page 111 and use perle cotton to stitch the vines and leaves. If you prefer hand embroidery to Big Stitch Quilting, refer to Embroidery Stitch Guide on page 108. Use two strands of floss and a stem stitch to stitch vines and leaves. Embellish the blocks with decorative stitches as desired.

A ski-lift ride provides a spectacular view of the Northwest country-side. Snow-capped peaks and endless sky create a picture-perfect scene.

HELPFUL HINT
We used a Bernina® artista 200E machine to embroider the berries and make decorative stitches.

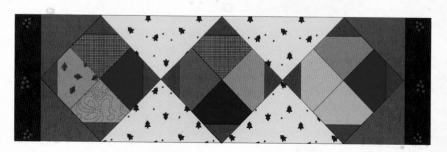

Berries and Vines Table Runner
Finished Size: 47" x 14"
Photo: page 70

**Berries and Vines Table Runner and Placemat
Embroidery Template**

Top Edge

Connect template
at dots

Trace one and
one reversed

Embroidery Lines ....
Placement Lines   — ·· — ·· —
Big Stitch Quilting Lines — — — —

Apple Tree Centerpiece

*Red and yellow apples, berries, and
boughs combine to make a charmingly
natural centerpiece.*

Apples peek among evergreen boughs to make
this striking centerpiece. A wire fruit stacker is
the key to this simple, yet sumptuous
centerpiece. Check with your local florist or
craft store for a fruit holder, or make your own
using heavy wire. Many people use a wooden
cone spiked with nails to hold the apples in a
cone shape. We prefer the fruit stacker as the
fruit is not damaged and can be eaten later, but
either form works well.

Place the fruit stacker on a glass cake plate
for height and drama. Place apples in the
spaces provided, saving the top spot for a
pillar candle. Use small pieces of cut greenery
to fill in the gaps between the apples. Add
holly or Oregon grape leaves and red berries
for even more interest. Use additional cut
greenery to line cake plate and add small
pinecones if desired.

To add even more sparkle, we surrounded
the apple tree with votive candles in pretty
glass holders.

Berries and Vines Placemats

Finished size: 20" x 14"

Accent your tablerunner and create a memorable table with these pretty placemats. Big Stitch vines and embroidered berries make these placemats extra special.

Fabric Requirements and Cutting Instructions

Read all instructions before beginning and use ¼"-wide seam allowances throughout.

Berries and Vines Placemats 20" x 14" For two placemats	FIRST CUT	
	Number of Strips or Pieces	Dimensions
Fabric A Center Square ⅜ yard	2	10½" squares
Fabric B First Border ¼ yard	4	2½" x 10½"
Fabric C Second Border ¼ yard	4	2½" x 14½"
Fabric D Outside Border ¼ yard	4	3½" x 14½"
Backing - ⅝ yard Batting - Two 22" x 16" pieces Embroidery Floss and Perle Cotton		

Making the Placemats

1. Sew 10½" Fabric A square between two 2½" x 10½" Fabric B pieces as shown. Press. Make two.

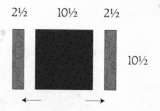

Make 2

2. Sew unit from step 1 between two 2½" x 14½" Fabric C pieces as shown. Press. Make two.

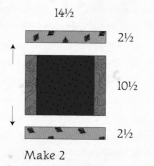

Make 2

3. Sew unit from step 2 between two 3½" x 14½" Fabric D pieces as shown. Press. Make two.

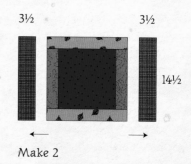

Make 2

4. Trace Berries and Vine Embroidery Template on page 73, marking placement lines. Refer to Embroidery Stitch Guide on page 108, photo, and layout. Use three strands of embroidery floss and a satin stitch to stitch berries.

5. Layer top and backing, right sides together, on batting. Using a ¼"-wide seam, stitch around edges leaving a 6" opening for turning. Trim batting close to stitching. Trim backing ¼" from seam line. Clip corners and turn. Press. Hand stitch opening closed.

6. Hand or machine quilt as desired. Refer to Big Stitch Quilting on page 111 and use perle cotton to quilt the vines and leaves. If you prefer embroidery to Big Stitch Quilting, refer to Embroidery Stitch Guide on page 108. Use two strands of embroidery floss and a stem stitch to embroider vines and leaves.

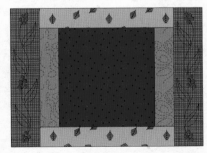

Berries and Vines Placemat
Finished Size: 20" x 14"
Photo: page 74

Show off the wonderful berries and vines embroidery on your placemats and create a new look for your table with these pretty accents.

Make 19" square napkins in a fabric to coordinate with the placemats. Simply hem the edges on all sides of the napkin and press. Fold the napkin diagonally to form a triangle. Starting from the bottom point, make even accordion pleats to the top edge. With the first pleat point facing away from you, fold the right point over the left one and tuck back through the loop created to form a loose knot. Tuck sprigs of real or faux berries, greenery, and twigs into one side of the knot.

For the other side of the knot, make botanical blessing cards. Textured handmade paper was torn to be approximately 2" x 3½". To tear paper, draw a 2" x 3½" rectangle on the back side of the paper. Using a paintbrush, wet the paper on the drawn line, allowing the paper to absorb the water. Place a cloth towel along the drawn line then place a ruler on top of the towel. Lifting toward you, use the ruler as a straight edge and tear the paper along the drawn line. Repeat for all sides. This procedure leaves soft edges on the paper.

Print blessings on vellum and trim vellum to approximately 1¼" x 3". Attach vellum to textured paper by setting eyelets in the four corners. Thread perle cotton through the eyelets to outline the blessing on all sides. Write a personalized blessing for each person or use our phrases.

Like stars in the night sky, may your holidays shine with joy and laughter.

May nature's beauty fill your heart with peace and serenity.

Holiday Pines Tree Skirt

Finished size: 46" round

I love to decorate with lots of pinecones and evergreen boughs during the holidays. The visual contrast between the soft greenery, the spiky cones, and red berries is especially pleasing in holiday arrangements. When it comes time to take the greenery down, I miss the lush colors and textures in my home. With this tree skirt, the rich wool pinecones and boughs will last forever and become an essential part of your holiday decorating.

Fabric Requirements

Read all instructions before beginning.

Holiday Pines Tree Skirt 46" diameter	Yardage
Fabric A Tree Skirt	1½ yards of 54"-wide fabric **OR** 2¾ yards 42"-wide fabric
Fabric B Pine Bough Background	1 yard
Pine Bough Appliqués	⅙ yard *each* of seven fabrics
Pinecone Appliqués	⅙ yard *each* of two fabrics
Pine Bur, Branch, and Berry Appliqués	Assorted Scraps

Backing - 2¾ yards
Tear-Away Stabilizer - 2 yards
Four-ply Yarn - 16 yards
Embroidery Thread or Floss and
 Perle Cotton
Yardstick Compass
Yardstick
Glue Stick
Buttons: twenty ⅜"

Making the Tree Skirt

The rich color and texture of felted wool make this tree skirt a holiday favorite. For information on felting wool refer to Tips for Appliquéing with Wool on page 64.

Assembly

We used 54"-wide wool for our tree skirt. To make top from 42"-wide fabric, cut 2¾ yards fabric in half crosswise. Sew pieces together to make one 48" x 81" (approximate) piece.

All appliqués are felt or felted wool fabric. If you prefer hand appliqué with cotton fabrics, refer to Hand Appliqué on page 109 and add ¼"-wide seam allowance to all appliqués.

1. To make 46½"-diameter circle pattern, place two yardstick compass points (available at quilt and craft shops) 23¼" apart on a yardstick. Draw 46½"-wide semi-circle on paper. Repeat process to make a 4" semi-circle center by placing compass points 2" apart on yardstick or ruler. Cut pattern on drawn lines.

2. Fold Fabric A in half. Place straight side of semi-circle pattern on fold. Cut tree skirt and circle for center hole. Stay stitch around 4" center circle by machine, ⅛" in from edge of fabric. Refer to layout on page 78 to make opening for tree skirt. Cut straight line from center circle to edge of tree skirt.

3. Referring to appliqué templates on page 47, trace patterns for eleven pinecones and burs, four of Pine Bough A and four reversed, thirteen of Pine Bough B, sixteen of Pine Bough C, and twenty-five berries.

4. Refer to page 79 to trace and make pattern for Pine Bough backgrounds. Cut four background sections from Fabric B. Fold Fabric B sections in half to mark centers with a pin. Fold tree skirt in fourths and mark with a pin. Referring to layout on page 78 and photo, pin three Fabric B sections to tree skirt centering Fabric B at pin marks 3" from edge of tree skirt. Cut remaining Fabric B section in half and pin on each side of tree skirt opening 3" from circular edge and even with straight edge. Place stabilizer on wrong side of tree skirt, making sure areas to be appliquéd have stabilizer under them.

5. Refer to page 47 and layout for pine bur placement. Use a glue stick to position pine burs on cones. Stitch burs to pinecones using a machine zig zag stitch or refer to Embroidery Stitch Guide on page 108 to stitch by hand, using two strands of embroidery floss and a blanket stitch.

6. Referring to layout on page 78 and photo, pin pinecones, pine boughs, and holly berries on Fabric B sections.

7. Refer to Embroidery Stitch Guide on page 108, layout on page 78, and photo. Stitch pinecones and pine boughs through all layers of tree skirt using a machine triple stitch or a hand running stitch. Attach berries with straight stitches in the shape of a pound sign (#) using perle cotton. Remove excess stabilizer.

8. Stitch Fabric B edges to tree skirt using four-ply yarn and large cross stitches.

9. Refer to Tree Skirt Embroidery Template, Embroidery Stitch Guide on page 108, photo on page 76, and layout. Stitch leaf designs between Fabric B sections with perle cotton using leaf stitch and chain stitches. Sew five ⅜" buttons at top of stem for berries or satin stitch berries.

10. Place tree skirt front and back right sides together. Machine stitch around tree skirt edges with a ¼"-wide seam, leaving 12" opening along one straight edge for turning. Clip corners and turn right side out. Gently press seams from wrong side of tree skirt. Stitch opening closed by hand or machine. Top stitch around edges of center circle for stability.

Finding just the right tree and cutting it down is a tradition for many Northwest families. Whether using a Forest Service permit or cutting a tree from their own property or at a tree farm, for many families the tree cutting expedition marks a joyful beginning to the holiday season.

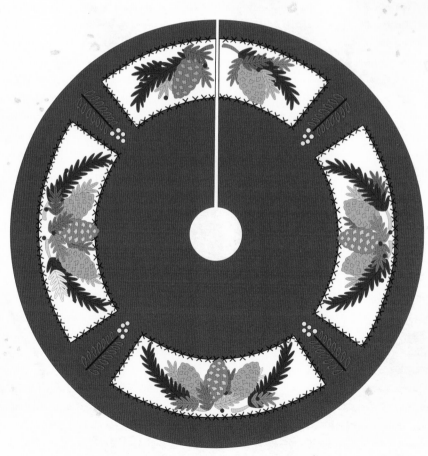

Holiday Pines Tree Skirt
Finished Size: 46" Round
Photo: page 74

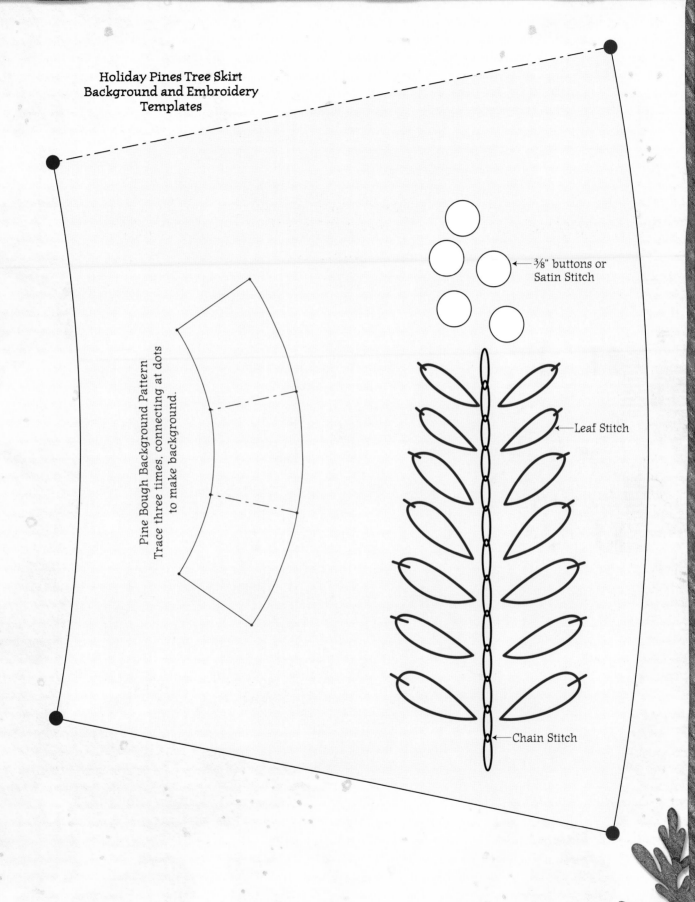

**Holiday Pines Tree Skirt
Background and Embroidery
Templates**

Pine Bough Background Pattern
Trace three times, connecting at dots
to make background.

⅜" buttons or
Satin Stitch

Leaf Stitch

Chain Stitch

Birds and Berries
Wool Ornaments

I keep a bird feeder outside, near my kitchen window, and enjoy watching the birds that come to feed all winter long. Last summer, a robin built a nest on a light fixture by the studio patio so we all got to watch the miracle of nature. Birds offer so much inspiration for my art and projects. These wool ornaments feature our feathered friends and berry branches.

Materials Needed:

Assorted colors of felted wool
Heavyweight fusible web
Perle cotton
Assorted buttons

Mistletoe and Bird

Holly Square

Cardinal

1. Refer to Quick-Fuse Appliqué on page 109 and Cardinal Templates. Trace and fuse the entire outline of cardinal and beak to 3½" x 6" wool backing. Trace, arrange, and fuse wing and head to cardinal. Refer to Embroidery Stitch Guide on page 108. Machine or hand stitch all edges of bird to wool backing using a blanket stitch. With perle cotton make a French knot to add an eye to bird. Add other decorative stitches as desired.

2. With pinking shears, cut backing about ³⁄₁₆" away from outline of bird. Make a hanging loop with 6" piece of perle cotton.

1. Follow instructions in step 1 of Cardinal Ornament to trace, fuse, and sew bird and branch to 4¾" circle background. Place leaves around branch and use a triple stitch by machine (or a stem stitch by hand) to stitch through center of leaves to attach to circle background.

2. Referring to photo and template, sew ¼" and ⅜" buttons to background for berries. Using a blanket stitch by hand or machine, sew background circle to 5½" backing. Trim backing with pinking shears about ³⁄₁₆" away from circle background. Make a hanging loop with 6" piece of perle cotton.

1. Refer to Embroidery Stitch Guide on page 108 and photo to satin stitch a holly branch to 3¾" wool background square. Trace and cut leaves from Holly Leaf Template. Position and pin holly leaves to background square. Use a triple stitch by machine (or stem stitch by hand) to sew stems and veins on holly leaves. Position and sew five ⅜" buttons on background for berries.

2. Position and pin ornament background to a 4½" accent square. With pinking shears, trim accent square ³⁄₁₆" away from background. Position and pin this unit to 5" backing square. With a blanket stitch, sew along edge of ornament background through all layers. Trim outside backing to within ³⁄₁₆" of accent square. Make a hanging loop with 6" piece of perle cotton.

Mistletoe and Bird Ornament

Birds and Berries Wool Ornament Appliqué Templates

Templates are reversed for use with Quick-Fuse Appliqué (page 109)

Cardinal Ornament

Holly Leaf
Cut 5

Frost gathers on the windowpanes and the wind whistles softly through the eaves. A freshly-made snowman leans on a broom outside the cabin door. Inside, the warmth is welcome after a full afternoon of snow sports. Upstairs the snowmen are snuggly, inviting the children to rest after a day of play.

Snowed In ...and loving it!

Snow Time Bed Quilt

Finished size: 68½" x 102½"

They may be made of snow, but they sure make me feel warm and cozy inside! Snowmen are among my favorite things and I celebrate these frosty folks in many of my paintings and projects. The snowmen on this quilt are loaded with charm with their Berber bodies and scarves flying in the wind. A flurry of snowflakes and playful red and white checks make this quilt a surefire kid pleaser!

Fabric Requirements and Cutting Instructions

Read all instructions before beginning and use ¼"-wide seam allowances throughout. Read Cutting Strips and Pieces on page 108 prior to cutting fabrics.

Snow Time Bed Quilt 68½" x 102½"	FIRST CUT		SECOND CUT	
	Number of Strips or Pieces	Dimensions	Number of Pieces	Dimensions
▨ Fabric A Background and Outside Border 4⅝ yards (directional)	2	166½" x 11¾" border*	2 2	79½" x 11¾" ** 45½" x 11¾" **
		Remove ½" of selvage, then cut borders. Some selvage may be in seam allowance.		
	2	73½" x 20" center*		
	4	8½" squares		
OR (non-directional) Center Panel and Corner Squares 2⅜ yards	1	73½" x 39½"		
	4	8½" squares		
Border 2⅜ yards	7	11¾" x 42"		
■ Fabric B Dark Checks and Corner Borders 1 yard	20	1½" x 42"	8 8	1½" x 11¾" 1½" x 9¾"
□ Fabric C Light Checks ¾ yard	15	1½" x 42"		
▨ Fabric D Corner Accent Border ⅙ yard	4	1⅛" x 42"	8 8	1⅛" x 9¾" 1⅛" x 8½"
▨ Fabric H Scarves Assorted scraps	7	1¾" x 17"		
Binding ¾ yard	9	2¾" x 42"		

Large Snowflakes - ¾ yard total of two fabrics
Medium Snowflakes - ⅙ yard
Snowmen - ½ yard Berber fleece or cotton fabric
Snowmen Arm, Mitten & Hat Appliqués - Assorted scraps
Lightweight Interfacing - 1 yard
Lightweight Fusible Web - 1¾ yards
Backing - 6⅛ yards
Batting - 75" x 109"
Embroidery Floss or Perle Cotton

*We used a border print, strips are cut lengthwise. For directional fabric, the measurement listed first runs parallel to selvage (strip width).
**You may wish to "fussy cut" for tree placement. See page 108.

Making the Center Panel

The Center Panel of this quilt is a whole cloth design. Seven assorted snowmen and assorted snowflakes are appliquéd to the center panel. A border print is used for the unique border treatment.

When using Berber fleece for snowmen appliqué pieces, fusible web is not recommended. Pin appliqués in place and stitch. To add extra interest to the quilt, use a different shade or contrasting thread for decorative stitches.

1. If using a border print, sew two 73½" x 20" Fabric A pieces together as shown to make 73½" x 39½" center panel. Press. For non-directional fabric, refer to Cutting Instructions.

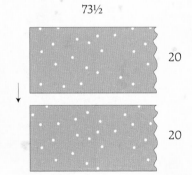

73½

20

20

2. The instructions given are for Quick-Fuse Appliqué. Referring to Quick-Fuse Appliqué on page 109, trace appliqué patterns on pages 90-91 for hats, mitten, and arms. Trace seven of the Large Snowflake Template on page 90 and five of Medium Snowflake Template on page 86.

If you prefer traditional hand appliqué, be sure to reverse all appliqué templates and add ¼"-wide seam allowances when cutting appliqué pieces. Refer to Hand Appliqué on page 109.

*The art of building a perfect
snowman is a pursuit that
begins in youth and continues
into adulthood because it
makes you feel young!*

3. Trace seven of each
snowman section from page 91
onto interfacing, leaving ½" space
between circles. Place traced
interfacing right sides together
with Berber fleece. Stitch on
traced lines. Cut out circles,
leaving ¼" seam allowance
(approximately) around each
circle. Slit interfacing in the
center of circle and turn circles
right side out. Finger-press edges.

4. With right sides together,
fold 1¾" x 17" Fabric H piece in
half lengthwise. Using ¼" seam
allowance, sew long edges
together. Turn right side out.
Make seven scarves.

5. Referring to photo on
page 84 and layout on page 89,
position and pin all appliqués.
Snowman circles are overlapped
½" to ¾". Mark position of
snowman circles and hats, then
remove temporarily. Fuse
snowflakes, arms, and mittens
in place. Finish snowflakes with
machine satin stitch, and finish
remaining fused appliqués with
a machine blanket stitch or
decorative stitching as desired.

6. Position and re-pin
snowman circles, scarves, and
hats. Fuse hats in place. Avoid
pressing fleece. Place center of
scarf behind snowman neck
then finish snowman circles
and hats with machine blanket
stitch or decorative stitching
as desired.

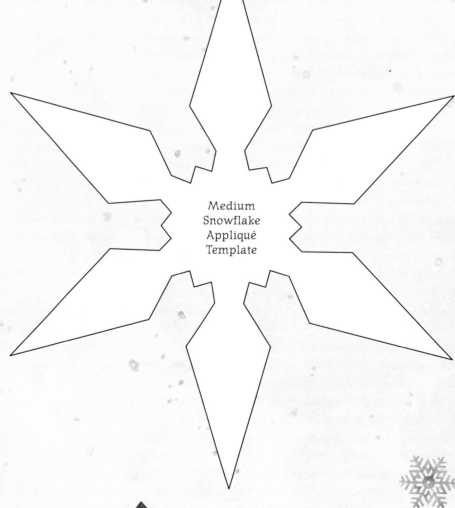

Medium
Snowflake
Appliqué
Template

7. Tie each scarf around snowman neck and tack in place at knot. Trim ends of each scarf to desired length. Use scissors to cut ½"-long fringe at both ends of scarf, if desired.

8. Refer to Embroidery Stitch Guide on page 108. Using perle cotton or six strands of floss, embroider French knot eyes and mouth, and satin-stitch nose on each Snowman Head.

Checked Border

Refer to Accurate Seam Allowance on page 108.

1. Sew five 1½" x 42" Fabric B strips and five 1½" x 42" Fabric C strips together as shown. Press seams toward dark fabrics. Make three strip sets.

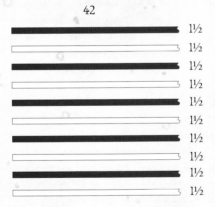

42

1½
1½
1½
1½
1½
1½
1½
1½
1½
1½

Make 3 sets

Finished Size: 36" x 26"

These snowflakes won't melt! Cubes of colors will keep these snowflakes in a deep freeze so you can lay your head on this pretty pillow. The perfect accent for the Snow Time Bed Quilt, this sham will add a finishing touch.

Materials Needed for One Sham

Fabric A Background - ½ yard
  Six 7½" squares
Fabric B Block Accent - ¼ yard
  Twelve 1" x 8½" pieces
  Twelve 1" x 7½" pieces
Fabric C Block Border - ⅜ yard
  Twelve 1½" x 10½" pieces
  Twelve 1½" x 8½" pieces
Fabric D Dark Checks - ⅛ yard
  Two 1½" x 15" strips
  One 1½" x 8" strip
Fabric E Light Checks - ⅛ yard
  One 1½" x 15" strip
  Two 1½" x 8" strips
Fabric F Outside Border - ½ yard
  Two 3½" x 30½" strips
  Two 3½" x 20½" strips
Lining and Batting - ⅞ yard
  39" x 29" piece of each
Backing - 1¼ yards
  Two 21" x 26½" pieces
Snowflake Appliqués - ½ yard*
Lightweight Fusible Web - ¾ yard*
*Optional

Making the Pillow Sham

1. Sew 7½" Fabric A square between two 1" x 7½" Fabric B pieces. Press. Make six. Sew this unit between two 1" x 8½" Fabric B pieces. Press. Make six.

2. Sew unit from step 1 between two 1½" x 8½" Fabric C pieces. Press. Make six. Sew this unit between two 1½" x 10½" Fabric C pieces. Press. Make six blocks.

1½   1½

10½

Make 6

3. Referring to photo, sew blocks together in two horizontal rows of three blocks each. Press seams in each row in opposite directions. Sew rows together. Press.

4. Sew unit from step 3 between two 3½" x 30½" Fabric F strips. Press.

5. Sew one 1½" x 15" Fabric E strip between two 1½" x 15" Fabric D strips. Press to dark fabric. Sew one 1½" x 8" Fabric D strip between two 1½" x 8" Fabric E strips. Press.

6. Cut eight 1½"-wide segments from the 15"-long set from step 5 as shown. From the 8"-long set, cut four 1½"-wide segments as shown. Sew together three segments as shown. Press. Make four checked units.

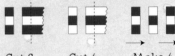

Cut 8   Cut 4   Make 4
segments   segments

7. Sew 3½" x 20½" Fabric F strip between two units from step 6. Press. Make two. Sew to sides. Press.

8. Refer to Quick-Fuse Appliqué on page 109, reduce Large Snowflake Template from page 90 by 80%. Trace, cut, position, and fuse six snowflakes on blocks. Finish with machine satin stitch or decorative stitching as desired.

9. Refer to Finishing Pillows on page 111. Quilt top and sew backing to pillow sham. Stitch-in-the-ditch between the Block Border and Outside Border to create a flange.

2. Cut strip sets from step 1 into seventy-two 1½"-wide segments.

1½

Cut seventy-two 1½" segments

3. Sew three segments together as shown. Press. Make twenty-four checked units.

Make 24

4. Sew together four checked units from step 3. Make two border rows. Using a seam ripper, remove one 1½"-wide, red-white-red segment from one end of each checked border row. Press. Referring to photo on page 84 and layout, sew checked borders to top and bottom of center panel. Press seams toward center panel.

Remove →

Make 2

5. Sew eight checked units from step 3 together. Press. Make two border rows. Using a seam ripper, remove one 1½"-wide, white-red-white segment from one end of each checked border row. Press. Referring to photo on page 84 and layout, sew borders to sides of center panel. Press seams toward center panel.

Make 2   ←Remove

Outside Border

1. If using <u>directional</u> border print fabric, refer to photo on page 84 and layout. Sew 45½" x 11¾" Outside Border pieces to top and bottom of quilt. Press seams toward borders.

For <u>non-directional</u> fabric, sew 11¾"-wide strips end-to-end. Cut two 45½" x 11¾" and two 79½" x 11¾" pieces.

2. Sew 8½" Fabric A square between two 1⅛" x 8½" Fabric D strips as shown. Press. Make four.

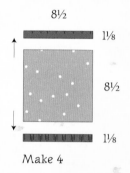

8½

1⅛

8½

1⅛

Make 4

3. Sew unit from step 2 between two 1⅛" x 9¾" Fabric D strips as shown. Press. Make four.

1⅛   1⅛

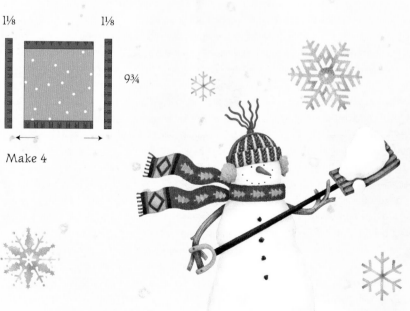

9¾

Make 4

4. Sew unit from step 3 between two 1½" x 9¾" Fabric B strips as shown. Press. Make four.

9¾

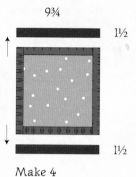

1½

1½

Make 4

5. Sew unit from step 4 between two 1½" x 11¾" Fabric B strips as shown. Press. Make four border corner units. Block measures 11¾" square.

1½   1½

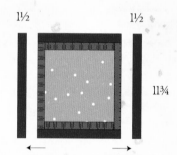

11¾

Make 4
Block measures 11¾" square

6. Referring to Quick-Fuse Appliqué on page 109 and using Large Snowflake Template on page 90, trace and cut out four snowflakes.

7. Position and fuse snowflakes on border corner units so two points are aligned with two corners of border as shown. Finish with machine satin stitch or decorative stitching as desired.

Make 4

8. Referring to photo on page 84 and layout, sew 79½" x 11¾" Outside Border strips between two blocks from step 7. Press seams toward borders. Make two. Sew to sides of quilt. Press seams toward borders.

Layering and Finishing

1. Cut backing fabric crosswise into two equal pieces and sew together to make one 75" x 109" (approximate) backing piece. Arrange and baste backing, batting, and top together, referring to Layering the Quilt on page 111.

2. Hand or machine quilt as desired.

3. Sew 2¾" x 42" binding strips end-to-end to make one continuous 2¾"-wide binding strip. Refer to Binding the Quilt on page 111, and bind quilt to finish.

Snow Time Bed Quilt
Finished Size: 68½" x 102½"
Photo: page 84

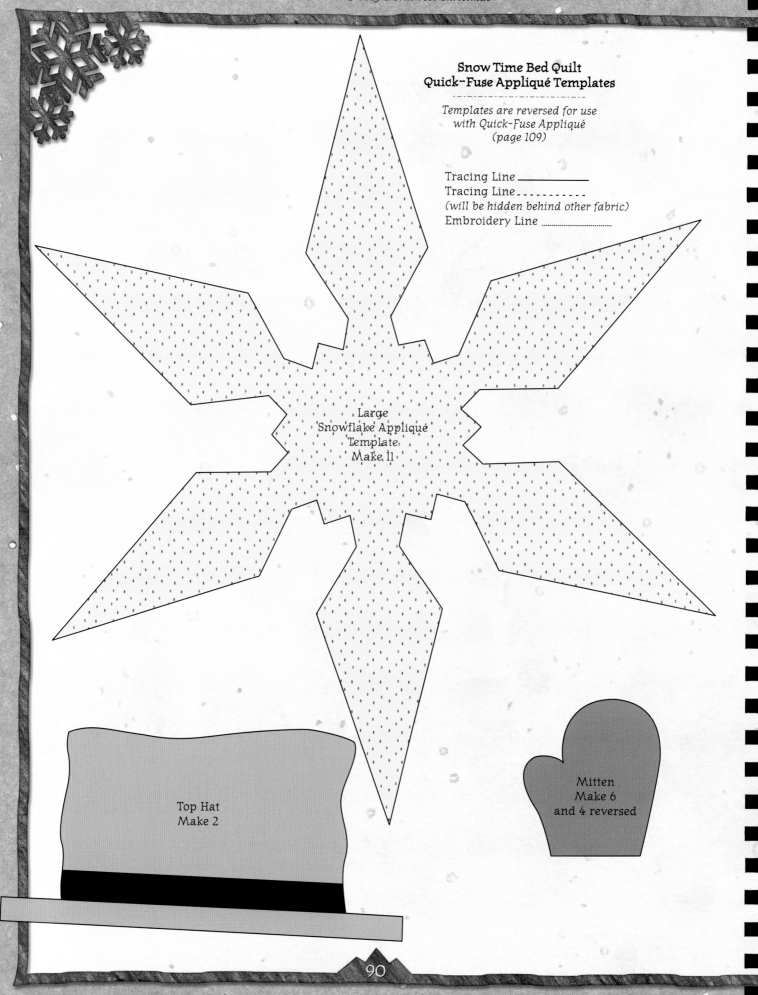

Snow Time Bed Quilt
Quick-Fuse Appliqué Templates

Templates are reversed for use
with Quick-Fuse Appliqué
(page 109)

Tracing Line _____
Tracing Line - - - - - - - - -
(will be hidden behind other fabric)
Embroidery Line ....

Large
Snowflake Appliqué
Template
Make 11

Top Hat
Make 2

Mitten
Make 6
and 4 reversed

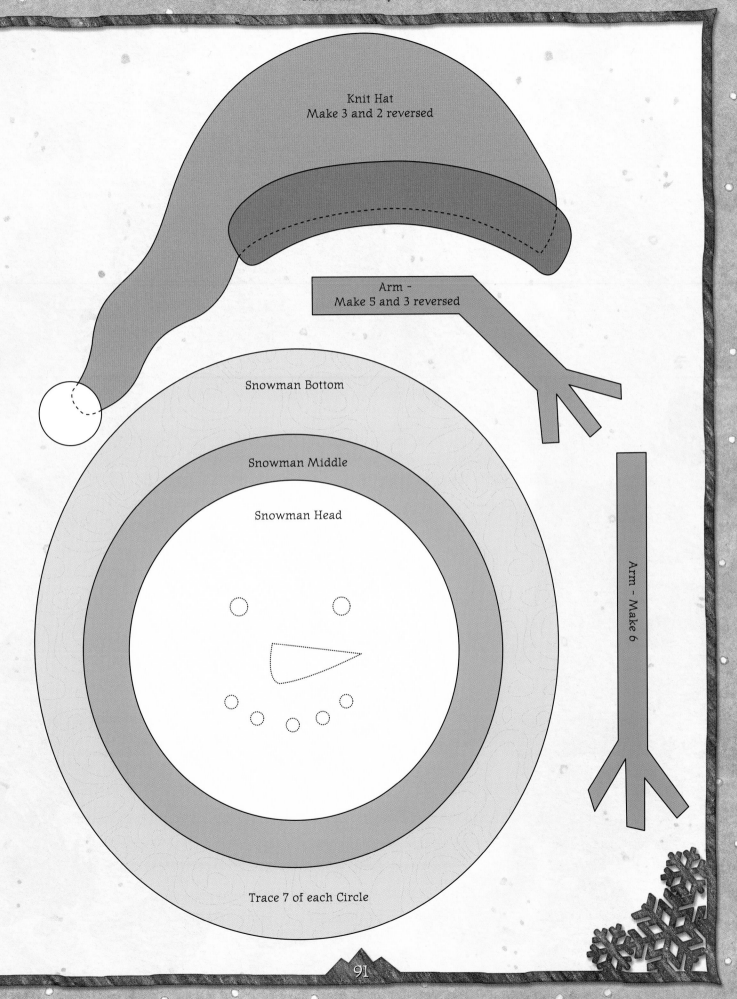

Knit Hat
Make 3 and 2 reversed

Arm -
Make 5 and 3 reversed

Snowman Bottom

Snowman Middle

Snowman Head

Arm - Make 6

Trace 7 of each Circle

Jingles the Snowman Pillow

Approximate Size: 11" x 17"

When the snow is perfect for packing, it's fun to watch the neighborhood come "alive" with new residents as snowmen appear on neighborhood lawns. Just like their makers, each frosty character has a distinct personality! Instead of the cold white stuff, our snuggly snowman is made of warm and cozy Berber. Jingle bells adorn his stocking cap and a colorful scarf and button eyes add even more personality to this friendly fellow.

Fabric and Materials Requirements

Snowman Body - ½ yard Berber fleece
Hat - ¼ yard double-sided fleece
  One 7" x 15" piece
Scarf - ¼ yard
  One 6" x 30½" piece
Nose Appliqué - Scrap
Buttons - two ⅝" and five ⁷⁄₁₆"
Perle Cotton - Red and black
Jingle Bells - 2
Polyester fiberfill
Compass and pencil

Making the Pillow

1. To make pattern, use a compass to draw 7½" and 11½" circles on paper or cardboard. Cut out circles and overlap 1¼" to join head and body. Pattern length is 17¾". Trace snowman pattern on wrong side of one half of Snowman Body fabric.

2. Fold traced fabric in half crosswise right sides together. Sew on traced line, leaving a 5" opening for turning and stuffing. Trim ¼" away from stitched line. Turn snowman body right side out.

3. Trace Nose Appliqué Template on wrong side of fabric scrap. Place traced fabric and a matching piece of fabric, right sides together, and stitch on traced line. Cut out nose leaving a ³⁄₁₆" seam allowance. Slit back of nose and turn right side out. Press. Refer to Embroidery Stitch Guide on page 108 and photo. Use perle cotton and a blanket stitch to sew nose to snowman's face.

4. Refer to photo to position and sew buttons to face, being careful not to catch the back fabric.

5. Softly stuff snowman body with polyester fiberfill as desired. Hand stitch opening closed.

6. Fold Scarf fabric lengthwise. Using ¼"-wide seam, stitch around all edges, leaving a 3" opening for turning. Turn scarf right side out, press, and hand stitch opening closed. Loosely tie around Snowman's neck.

7. Fold hat fabric in half crosswise and stitch along 7" edge using a ¼"-wide seam. Referring to photo, gather one raw edge of hat and tie four strands of perle cotton around gathers about 1½" from edge to form top of hat. Tie on bells and finish with a bow. Use perle cotton to blanket stitch remaining edge of hat. Turn up blanket-stitched edge to form cuff on hat and place at an angle on Snowman's head.

Nose

Jingles the Snowman Pillow
Appliqué Template

Snow Fun Wall Quilt

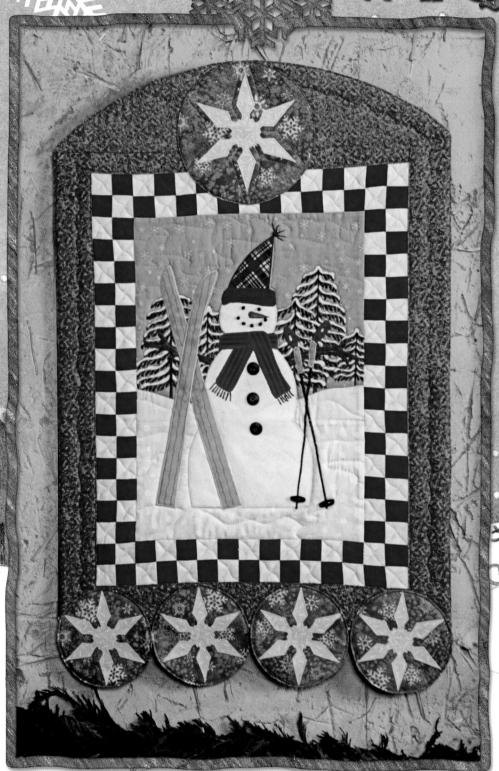

Finished size:
19" x 29"

When you live in snow country, you find lots of ways to enjoy the snow! I still feel that child-like excitement when we get the first snowfall of the season. I'm tempted to run right outside to make snow angels or don cross-country skis. I hope I never outgrow that enchanted feeling. With its unique shape and border detail our skiing snowman quilt celebrates that joy and will slide right into your heart.

Fabric Requirements and Cutting Instructions

Read all instructions before beginning and use ¼"-wide seam allowances throughout.

Snow Fun Wall Quilt 19" x 29"	FIRST CUT	
	Number of Strips or Pieces	Dimensions
Fabric A Sky ⅜ yard	1	11½" x 10"
We "fussy cut" a border print*		
Fabric B Snow ¼ yard	1	11½" x 6"
Fabric C Light Checks ¼ yard	3	1½" x 42"
Fabric D Dark Checks ¼ yard	3	1½" x 42"
Fabric E Snowflake Background ½ yard	2	7" x 42"
Outside Border ⅓ yard	1	5" x 20"
	2	2½" x 22½"
	1	2½" x 15½"
	1	1½" x 15½"

Snowman, Skis, Poles, Hat and Scarf
  Appliqués - Assorted scraps
Backing - ⅔ yard
Batting - 23" x 27" and 7" x 42"
Lightweight Fusible Web - ⅓ yard
Beads and Buttons
Embroidery Floss

*You may wish to "fussy cut" for sky placement. See page 108.

Making the Center Panel

1. Sew 11½" x 10" Fabric A piece to 11½" x 6" Fabric B piece. Press.

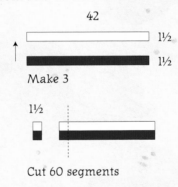

2. Sew 1½" x 42" Fabric C strip to 1½" x 42" Fabric D strip as shown. Press. Make three sets. Cut sixty 1½"-wide segments from sets as shown.

Make 3

Cut 60 segments

3. Sew two 1½"-wide segments from step 2 together as shown. Press. Make twenty-eight.

Make 28

4. Sew two units from step 3 together as shown. Press. Make twelve.

Make 12

5. Sew two units from step 4, one unit from step 3, and one unit from step 2 together as shown. Press. Make two.

Make 2

6. Sew four units from step 4, one unit from step 3, and one unit from step 2 together as shown. Press. Make two.

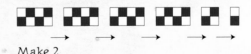

Make 2

7. Referring to layout on page 97 and photo, sew units from step 5 to top and bottom of center panel. Press seams toward center panel. Sew units from step 6 to sides of center panel. Press.

8. Referring to layout on page 97 and photo, sew 1½" x 15½" Outside Border strip to top of quilt and 2½" x 15½" Outside Border strip to bottom of quilt. Press toward border.

9. Referring to layout on page 97 and photo, sew two 2½" x 22½" Outside Border strips to sides of quilt. Press seams toward border.

10. Trace Top Curve Pattern from page 98, adding ¼" seam allowance at stitch lines. Place pattern on crosswise folded 5" x 20" Outside Border strip and cut one. Sew to top of quilt as shown. Press.

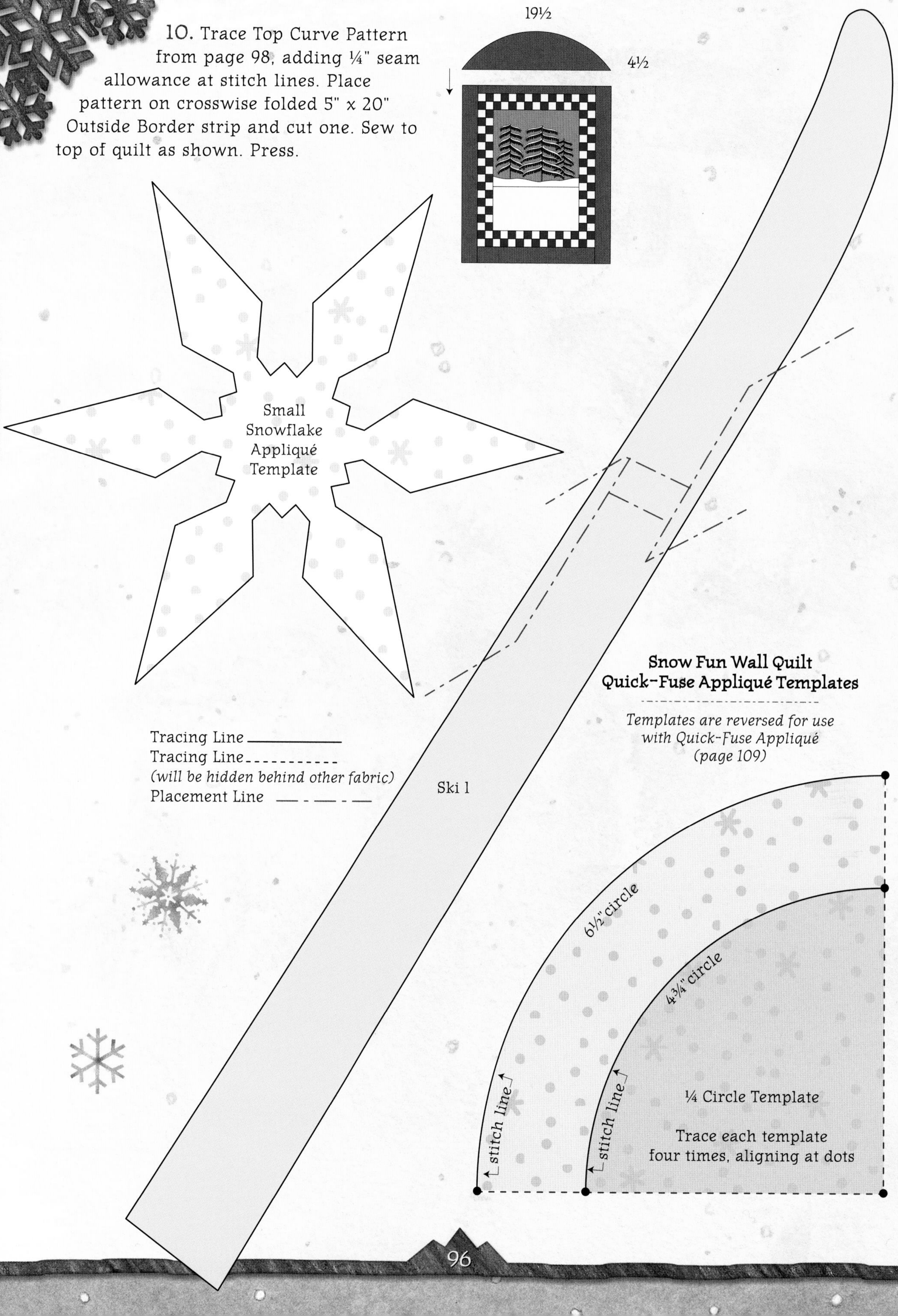

19½

4½

Small Snowflake Appliqué Template

Tracing Line ——————
Tracing Line ------------
(will be hidden behind other fabric)
Placement Line — · — · —

Ski 1

**Snow Fun Wall Quilt
Quick-Fuse Appliqué Templates**

*Templates are reversed for use
with Quick-Fuse Appliqué
(page 109)*

6½" circle

4¾" circle

stitch line

stitch line

¼ Circle Template

Trace each template
four times, aligning at dots

Adding the Appliqués

The instructions given are for Quick-Fuse Appliqué. If you prefer traditional hand appliqué, be sure to reverse all appliqué templates and add ¼" seam allowances when cutting appliqué pieces. Refer to Hand Appliqué directions on page 109.

1. Referring to Quick-Fuse Appliqué on page 109, trace appliqué templates on pages 86, 96, 98, and 99 for snowman, arms, hat, skis, ski pole tops, and one medium and four small snowflakes.

2. Referring to photo on page 94 and layout, position and fuse snowman and accessories to center panel. Machine satin stitch ski poles and finish appliqués with machine satin stitch or decorative stitching as desired.

3. Referring to Embroidery Stitch Guide on page 108 and photo on page 94, use three strands of embroidery floss and a stem stitch to embroider fringe at top of hat and ends of scarf.

Layering and Finishing

1. Layer backing and quilt top, right sides together, on batting. Stitch around edges, using a ¼"-wide seam allowance, and leaving a 6" opening on one side for turning. Trim batting and backing, turn, and press. Hand stitch opening closed.

2. Machine or hand quilt as desired.

3. Make circle patterns by tracing 4¾" and 6½" circles from page 96. Trace one 6½" circle and four 4¾" circles on wrong side of one Fabric E strip, leaving ½" between circles. Place Fabric E strips, right sides together, on top of a matching-size piece of batting. Stitch on drawn lines. Cut out circles, leaving ¼" seam allowance. Clip curves. Slit the back circle as shown and turn right side out. Press.

4. Referring to Quick-Fuse Appliqué on page 109 and layout, fuse medium snowflake appliqué on large circle and four small snowflakes on smaller circles. Finish with machine satin stitch or decorative stitching as desired. Tack large circle at top of quilt, overlapping checked border and placing two points of snowflake vertically. Tack four small circles at bottom of quilt, overlapping outside border and placing snowflake points vertically.

5. Referring to photo on page 94 and layout, add beads for eyes, mouth, and top of hat, and oval beads at bottom of ski poles. Sew buttons as shown.

Snow Fun Wall Quilt
Finished Size: 19" x 29"
Photo: page 94

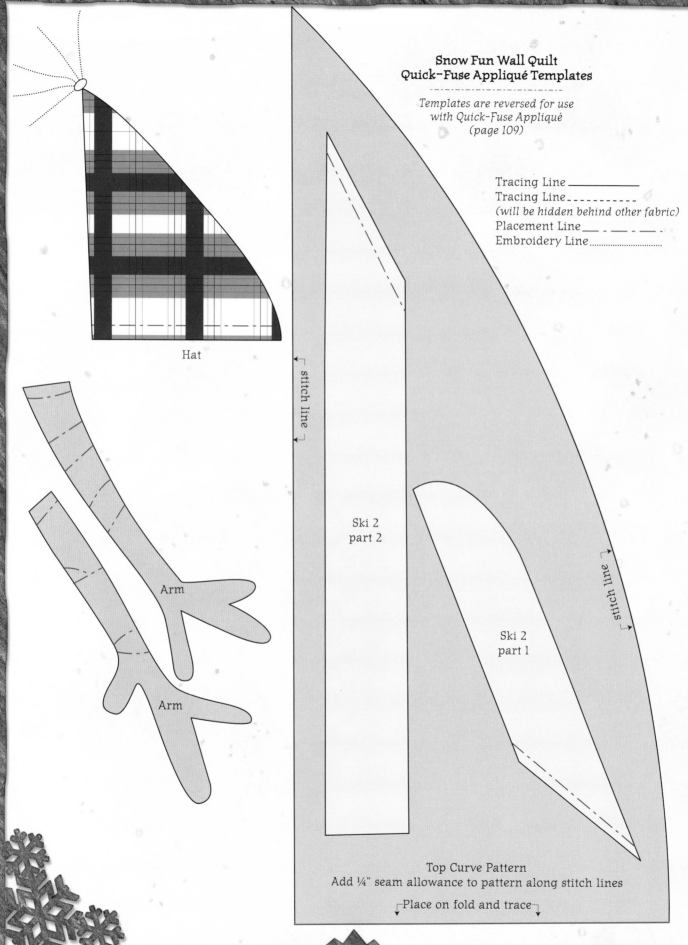

Hat

Arm

Arm

Snow Fun Wall Quilt
Quick-Fuse Appliqué Templates

Templates are reversed for use
with Quick-Fuse Appliqué
(page 109)

Tracing Line ——————
Tracing Line ------------
(will be hidden behind other fabric)
Placement Line __ . __ . __ .
Embroidery Line ....

stitch line

Ski 2
part 2

stitch line

Ski 2
part 1

Top Curve Pattern
Add ¼" seam allowance to pattern along stitch lines

Place on fold and trace

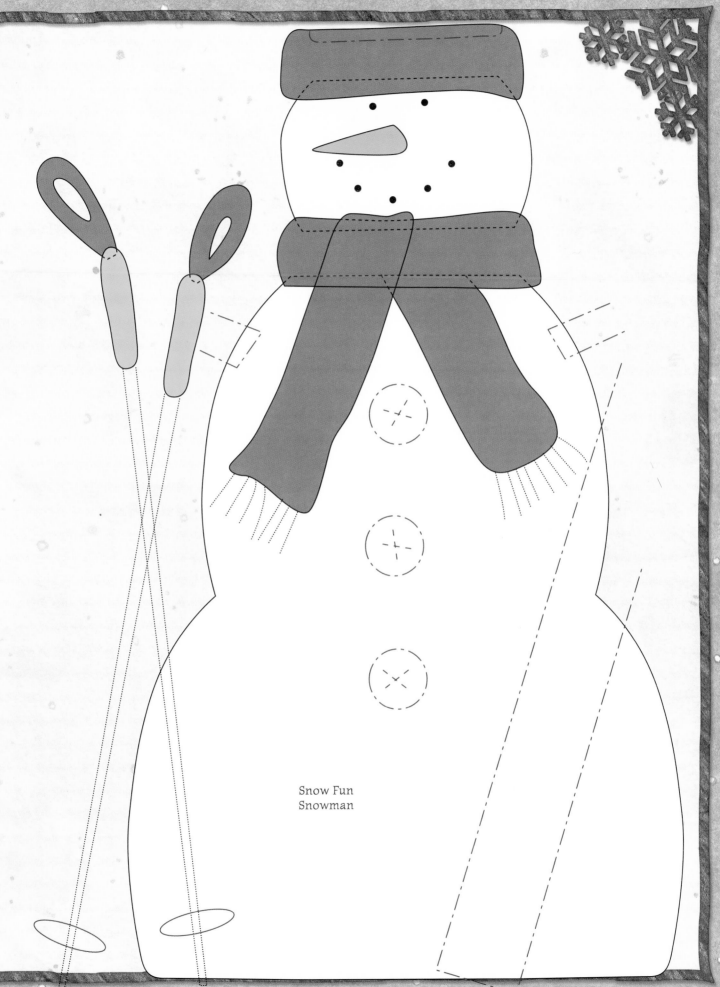

Snow Fun
Snowman

Making Merry Wall Art

When a fresh snowfall blankets my hometown the "white-stuff" magically
transforms it into a whole new world—fresh, clean, lit-up, and inviting you to come
out to play. Neighborhood kids careen down hills on their sleds and ice skaters
glide on frozen ponds. Two good-time snowmen make merry in a winter
wonderland in these fanciful framed wall pieces. Forever frozen in wintertime
fun, these snowmen are sure to be seasonal decorating favorites!

Materials Needed

Unfinished wood frames
*(we used frames with 12" x 10"
and 9" x 9" openings)*
Wood sealer
Acrylic paints in light and
medium blue, ivory
Matte spray varnish
Ceramic Snowflake buttons *(Optional)*
Hot glue gun and sticks
Assorted paintbrushes
Old toothbrush
Sea sponge
Fine sandpaper
Push points
Picture hangers
Snowman Background Fabric -
Measurement determined in
Step 1
Snowman Appliqués -
Assorted scraps
Batting - Assorted scraps
Heavyweight Fusible Web - ¼ yard
Embroidery floss
Beads
Spray adhesive

Painting the Frames

1. Sand unfinished wood frame if needed. Use paintbrush to apply wood sealer and allow to dry. If grain is raised, sand lightly.

2. Basecoat frames with medium blue paint. Allow paint to dry thoroughly between all steps.

3. Dampen sea sponge and wring well. Dip in medium then light blue paint colors and blot on paper towel. Using a tapping motion, sponge paint onto frame, applying lightly for a mottled effect.

4. When dry, add ivory spatters to frame. Mix a small amount of water with ivory paint, fill an old toothbrush with this mixture then rub thumb over the bristles to spatter. Practice this technique on a piece of paper before trying it on frame. If the paint is watered down too much, spatters will blend with the sponging rather than standing out like snow.

5. When thoroughly dry, spray frames with matte varnish. Hot glue snowflake buttons to frame, if desired.

Making the Panels

1. On wrong side of frame, measure the maximum opening including the rabbet (grooved edge). Cut a piece of cardboard ⅛" smaller in both width and height. The background fabric measurement will need to be 3" larger than the cardboard size. To add an extra element to background, sew a 3"-5" fabric strip for snow, then cut pieced background to background fabric measurement.

2. Referring to Quick-Fuse Appliqué on page 109, trace snowmen on pages 102-103. Arrange and fuse to background fabric.

3. Referring to photo and Embroidery Stitch Guide on page 108, use embroidery floss and a stem stitch to add scarf and hat fringe to snowman panels. Add bead embellishments as desired.

4. Cut batting the same size as cardboard. Use spray adhesive to attach batting to cardboard.

5. Place snowman panel on batting, wrap to back of cardboard, and tape or glue in place.

6. Place snowman panel in painted frame. Secure in place with push points and attach hanger. Finish with additional cardboard or craft paper, if desired.

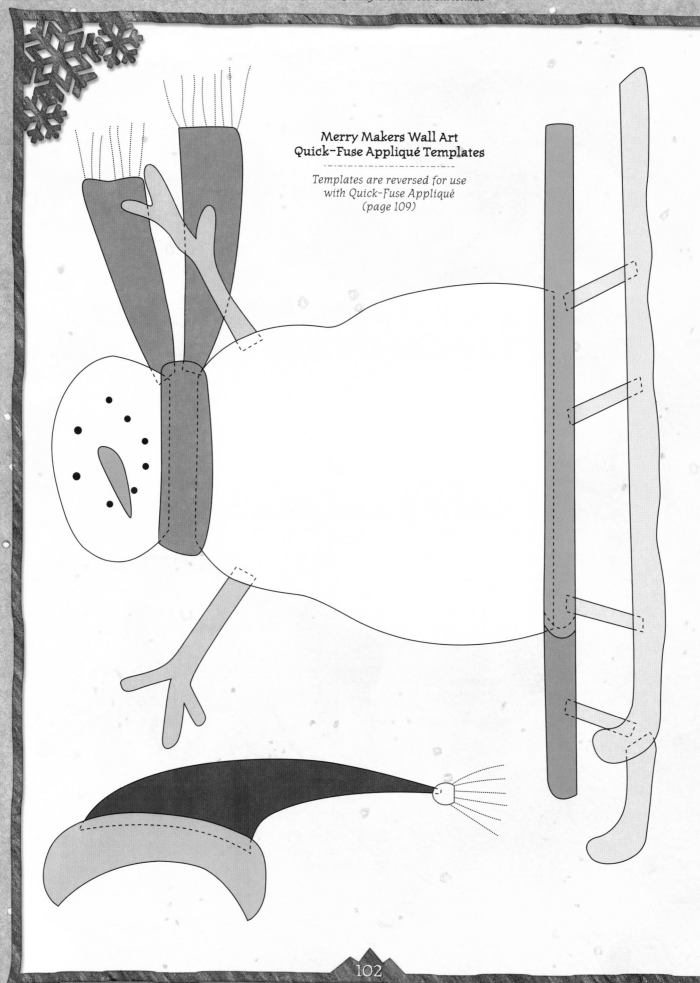

Merry Makers Wall Art
Quick-Fuse Appliqué Templates

Templates are reversed for use
with Quick-Fuse Appliqué
(page 109)

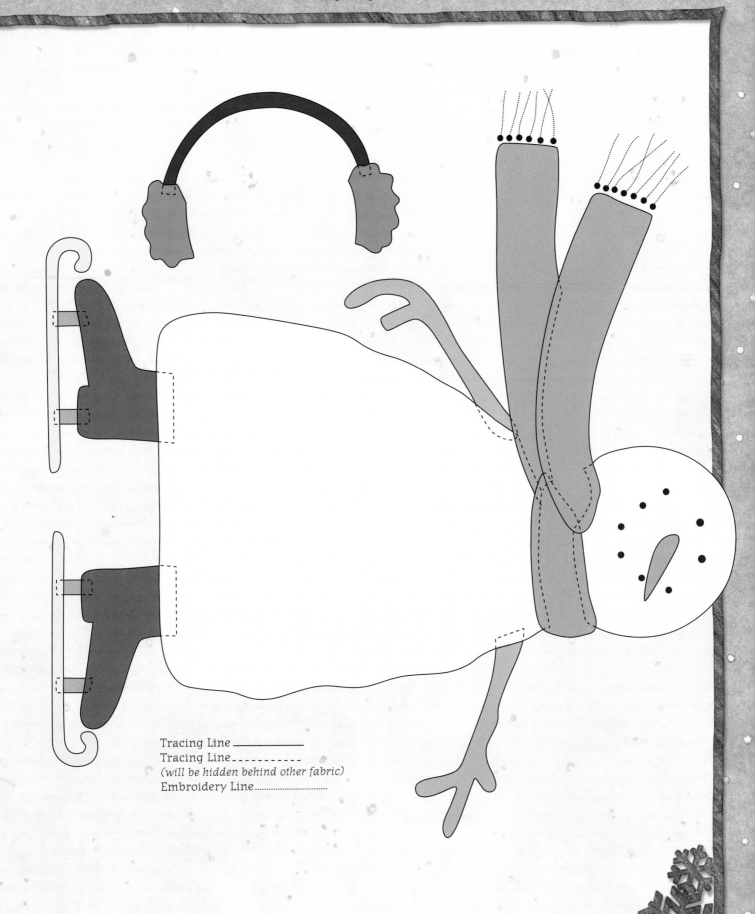

Tracing Line _____
Tracing Line - - - - - - - - - - -
(will be hidden behind other fabric)
Embroidery Line ....

Snow Flurry
Chenille Pillow

Finished size:
19¼" x 19¼"

Few things are more beautiful than sunshine on new-fallen snow. It reminds me of my early craft projects filled with glue and glitter. This chenille pillow is reminiscent of a crisp winter day with a bright blue sky and the sun glittering the snow. A few lazy snowflakes still drift in the air, but instead of being chilly, this pillow is comfy cozy!

Fabric Requirements and Cutting Instructions

Read all instructions before beginning and use ¼"-wide seam allowances throughout. Read Cutting Strips and Pieces on page 108 prior to cutting fabrics.

Snow Flurry Chenille Pillow 19¼" x 19¼"	FIRST CUT		SECOND CUT	
	Number of Strips or Pieces	Dimensions	Number of Pieces	Dimensions
Chenille Layers Fabric A Fabric B Fabric C Fabric D Fabric E Fabric F Fabric G ¼ yard each of seven fabrics	1*	6½" x 42" *cut for each of seven fabrics*	4* 2*	7" squares 5½" squares
Fabric H Snowflake Background ¼ yard	1	6½" x 42"	4	6½" squares
Accent Border ⅛ yard	2	1⅛" x 42"	2 2	1⅛" x 19¾" 1⅛" x 18½"
Pillow Backing ½ yard	1	12¾" x 42"	2	12¾" x 19¾"

Snowflake Appliqué - ⅙ yard Berber fleece
Pillow Form - 19¼"
Pom-pom Trim - 2¼ yards
Temporary Spray Adhesive

MAKE IT EASY!

To make cutting between seam lines easier and more accurate, check your local quilt shop for mini-strip cutting mats. These long, narrow self-healing mats are simple to insert between two seam lines, enabling one to rotary cut several layers of fabric at once with precision.

Making Chenille Fabric

1. Mark a diagonal line from corner to corner on wrong side of 7" Fabric G square. Continue to mark parallel lines ⅝" apart from first drawn line until entire piece is marked. Layer 7" Fabric A, B, C, D, E, F, and G squares on top of each another, right sides down. We used four white fabrics (C, D, E and F) and three medium blue fabrics (A, B and G). Pin layers in place. Sew on marked diagonal lines through all layers. Make four squares.

Make 4

2. Place square from step 1 right side up. Cut top six layers of fabrics between stitched lines, leaving Fabric G intact.

When the wonderful white stuff covers our community, we head to local parks and recreation areas for some good old-fashioned sledding fun.

3. Several techniques can be used to make Chenille fabric. Following manufacturer's instructions, use a chenille tool that looks like a large toothbrush with stiff bristles to roughen fabric. Another technique is to immerse squares in water, wring out water, fold squares in half, and rub fabrics back and forth against each another. Allow to dry. A third option is to immerse squares in water then place in dryer with other clean items on medium setting for fifteen minutes. After fabrics have been roughened, squares can be trimmed to desired sizes. This helps to make sure that the chenille look will extend all the way to the seams in finished project.

4. Square chenille to 6½" x 6½", making sure center stitch line is at a 45° angle.

5. Repeat steps 1, 2, and 3 with 5½" Fabric A, B, C, D, E, F, and G squares. Make two. Square to 5⅛".

Make 2
Square to 5⅛"

6. Cut both chenille squares from step 5 in half diagonally as shown for a total of four triangles. Sew two triangles together as shown. Make two. Press seams open. Sew joined triangle pairs together. Press. Square to 6½".

Make 2   Square to 6½"

Snowflake Squares

When using Berber fleece, as we did, for Snowflake appliqués, use spray adhesive or pins to hold appliqués in place. To quick-fuse or hand appliqué snowflakes, refer to page 109.

Trace and cut four snowflakes using Medium Snowflake Template on page 86. Position snowflake on 6½" Fabric H square. Finish appliqué edges with machine satin stitch or decorative stitching as desired. Make four.

6½

 6½

Make 4

Pillow Assembly

1. Sew Snowflake Square between two chenille squares from step 4 as shown. Press. Make two.

Make 2

2. Sew pieced chenille square from step 6 between two appliquéd snowflake squares as shown. Press.

3. Sew row from step 2 between rows from step 1 as shown.

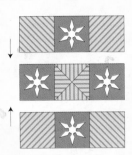

4. Referring to photo on page 104 and layout, sew 1⅛" x 18½" Accent Border strips to top and bottom of pillow. Press toward border.

5. Sew 1⅛" x 19¾" Accent Border strips to sides of pillow. Press.

Finishing

1. Baste pom-pom trim to right side of pillow top, making sure that pom-pom tape will be enclosed in the seam.

2. Refer to Finishing Pillows and Pillow Forms on page 111, steps 2-4 to finish pillow.

Snow Flurry Chenille Pillow
Finished Size: 19¼" x 19¼"
Photo: page 104

Finished Size: 19" long

Who could resist these whimsical stockings? A Chenille technique makes them cozy, bells and pom-poms make them merry!

Silver Bells Stocking

(stocking on right)

Materials Needed

Stocking front - ½ yard each of seven fabrics
   Three 4" x 40" strips for each of seven fabrics
Stocking back - ⅝ yard
Cuff - ⅓ yard
   One 8½" x 16" strip
Snowflake appliqué - scrap
Lining - ⅓ yard
Rickrack trim- ½ yard
Lightweight fusible web - scrap
Assorted silver bells

1. Refer to Snow Flurry Chenille Pillow page 105-106, steps 1 through 3, to make 4" x 40" chenille strip. Sew 45° diagonal lines ⅝" apart on strip. Make three. Cut thirty 3½" squares from roughened chenille strips.

2. Refer to Making the Stocking Pattern on page 51. Refer to photo and pattern to position and sew chenille squares together. Press seams open.

3. Refer to Forest Friends Stocking page 51, steps 5 through 7, to sew stocking, lining, and cuff. Refer to Quick-Fuse Appliqué on page 109 and Small Snowflake Template on page 96 to fuse and sew snowflake to cuff. Refer to step 8 on page 51 to sew cuff to stocking.

Snowball Stocking

(stocking on left)

Materials Needed

Stocking and Lining - ⅓ yard each
Chenille Cuff - ⅛ yard each of seven fabrics
   One 4" x 20" strip each of seven fabrics
Cuff Accent - ⅙ yard Berber Fleece
   One 4½" x 16" strip
Snowflake, Heel and Toe Appliqués - Berber fleece scraps
Rickrack trim - 1 yard
Pom-pom trim - ½ yard
Lightweight Fusible web - ⅙ yard

1. Refer to Making the Stocking Pattern and Forest Friends Stocking page 51, steps 1 and 2, to quilt stocking and appliqué heel and toe pieces. Refer to photo and Snow Flurry Chenille Pillow, Snowflake Squares, page 106, to make, trace, and appliqué snowflake to stocking.

2. Refer to Snow Flurry Chenille Pillow pages 105-106, steps 1-3, to make 4" x 20" chenille strip. Sew 45° diagonal lines ⅝" apart. Cut six 3½" squares from roughened chenille strip.

3. Refer to photo to sew chenille squares together. Press seams open. Cut strip to 3½" x 16".

4. Baste pom-pom trim to right side of cuff, making sure that pom-pom tape will be enclosed in seam.

5. With right sides together sew short ends of chenille strip together. Press seam open.

6. With right sides together, sew short ends of 4½" x 16" cuff accent strip together. Press. Fold strip in half lengthwise. Place folded strip on top of pom-pom tape matching raw edges, and sew to cuff. Finger press. Sew rickrack trim to cuff.

7. Refer to Forest Friends Stocking page 51, steps 5 through 8 to complete stocking.

General Directions

Cutting Strips and Pieces

Before you make each of the projects in this book, pre-wash and press the fabrics. Using a rotary cutter, see-through ruler, and a cutting mat, cut the strips and pieces for the project. If indicated on the Cutting Chart, some will need to be cut again into smaller strips and pieces. Make second cuts in order shown to maximize use of fabric. The approximate width of the fabric is 42". Measurements for all pieces include ¼"-wide seam allowance unless otherwise indicated. Press in the direction of the arrows.

Fussy Cut

To make a "fussy cut", carefully position ruler or template over a selected design in fabric. Include seam allowances before cutting designated pieces.

Assembly Line Method

Whenever possible, use the assembly line method. Position pieces right sides together and line up next to sewing machine. Stitch first unit together, then continue sewing others without breaking threads. When all units are sewn, clip threads to separate. Press in direction of arrows.

Accurate Seam Allowance

Accurate seam allowances are always important, but especially when the quilt top contains multiple pieced borders with lots of blocks and seams! If each seam is off as little as ¹⁄₁₆", you'll soon find yourself struggling with components that just won't fit. To ensure you are stitching a perfect ¼"-wide seam, try this simple test.

Cut three strips of fabric, each exactly 1½" x 12". With right sides together, and long raw edges aligned, sew two strips together, carefully maintaining a ¼" seam. Press. Add the third strip to complete the strip set. Press seams to one side and measure. The finished strip set should measure 3½" x 12". The center strip should measure 1"-wide, the two outside strips 1¼"-wide, and the seam allowances exactly ¼". If your measurements differ, check to make sure that you have pressed the seams flat. If your strip set still doesn't "measure up," try stitching a new strip set, adjusting the seam allowance until you are able to achieve a perfect ¼"-wide seam.

Quick Corner Triangles

Quick corner triangles are formed by simply sewing fabric squares to other squares or rectangles. The directions and diagrams with each project illustrate what size pieces to use and where to place squares on the corresponding piece. Follow steps 1–3 below to make quick corner triangle units.

1. With pencil and ruler, draw diagonal line on wrong side of fabric square that will form the triangle. See Diagram A. This will be your sewing line.

2. With right sides together, place square on corresponding piece. Matching raw edges, pin in place, and sew ON drawn line. Trim off excess fabric, leaving ¼" seam allowance as shown in Diagram B.

3. Press seam in direction of arrow as shown in step-by-step project diagram. Measure completed corner triangle unit to ensure the greatest accuracy.

A.   sewing line

B.   trim ¼" away from sewing line

C.   finished quick corner triangle unit

Embroidery Stitch Guide

Stem Stitch

Satin Stitch

French Knot

Herringbone Stitch

Feather Stitch

Cretan Stitch

Blanket Stitch

Leaf Stitch

Overcast Stitch

Cross Stitch

Quick-Fuse Appliqué

Quick-fuse appliqué is a method of adhering appliqué pieces to a background with fusible web. For quick and easy results, simply quick-fuse appliqué pieces in place. Use sewable, lightweight fusible web for the projects in this book unless otherwise indicated. Finishing raw edges with stitching is desirable; laundering is not recommended unless edges are finished.

1. With paper side up, lay fusible web over appliqué design. Leaving ½" space between pieces, trace all elements of design. Cut around traced pieces, approximately ¼" outside traced line. See Diagram A.

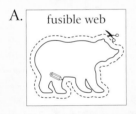

A. fusible web

2. With paper side up, position and iron fusible web to wrong side of selected fabrics. Follow manufacturer's directions for iron temperature and fusing time. Cut out each piece on traced line. See Diagram B.

B. fabric-wrong side

3. Remove paper backing from pieces. A thin film will remain on wrong side of fabric. Position and fuse all pieces of one appliqué design at a time onto background, referring to photos for placement. Fused design will be the reverse of traced pattern.

Appliqué Pressing Sheet

An appliqué pressing sheet is very helpful when there are many small elements to apply using a quick-fuse appliqué technique. The pressing sheet allows small items to be bonded together before applying them to the background. The sheet is coated with a special material that prevents the fusible web from adhering permanently to the sheet. Follow manufacturer's directions. Remember to let the fabric cool completely before lifting it from the appliqué sheet. If not cooled, the fusible web could remain on the sheet instead of on the fabric.

Machine Appliqué

This technique should be used when you are planning to launder quick-fuse projects. Several different stitches can be used: small narrow zig zag stitch, satin stitch, blanket stitch, or another decorative machine stitch. Use an appliqué foot if your machine has one. Use a stabilizer to obtain even stitches and help prevent puckering. Always practice first to check your machine settings.

1. Fuse all pieces following Quick-Fuse Appliqué directions.

2. Cut a piece of stabilizer large enough to extend beyond the area you are stitching. Pin to the wrong side of fabric.

3. Select thread to match appliqué.

4. Following the order that appliqués were positioned, stitch along the edges of each section. Anchor beginning and ending stitches by tying off or stitching in place two or three times.

5. Complete all stitching, then remove stabilizers.

Hand Appliqué

Hand appliqué is easy when you start out with the right supplies. Cotton or machine embroidery thread is easy to work with. Pick a color that matches the appliqué fabric as closely as possible. Use appliqué or silk pins for holding shapes in place and a long, thin needle, such as a sharp, for stitching.

1. Make a template for every shape in the appliqué design. Use a dotted line to show where pieces overlap.

2. Place template on right side of appliqué fabric. Trace around template.

3. Cut out shapes ¼" beyond traced line.

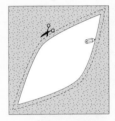

4. Position shapes on background fabric, referring to quilt layout. Pin shapes in place.

5. When layering and stitching appliqué shapes, always work from background to foreground. Where shapes overlap, do not turn under and stitch edges of bottom pieces. Turn and stitch the edges of the piece on top.

6. Use the traced line as your turn-under guide. Entering from the wrong side of the appliqué shape, bring the needle up on the traced line. Using the tip of the needle, turn under the fabric along the traced line. Using blind stitch, stitch along the folded edge to join the appliqué shape to the background fabric. Turn under and stitch about ¼" at a time.

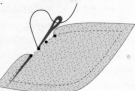

Adding the Borders

1. Measure quilt through the center from side to side. Trim two border strips to this measurement. Sew to top and bottom of quilt. Press toward border.

2. Measure quilt through the center from top to bottom, including borders added in step 1. Trim border strips to this measurement. Sew to sides and press. Repeat to add additional borders.

Making Bias Strips

1. Refer to Fabric Requirements and Cutting Instructions for the amount of fabric required for the specific bias needed.

2. Remove selvages from the fabric piece and cut into a square. Mark edges with straight pin where selvages were removed as shown. Cut square once diagonally into two equal 45° triangles. (For larger squares, fold square in half diagonally and gently press fold. Open fabric square and cut on fold.)

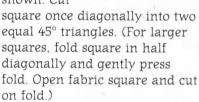

3. Place pinned edges right sides together and stitch along edge with a ¼" seam. Press seam open.

4. Using a ruler and rotary cutter, cut bias strips to width specified in quilt directions.

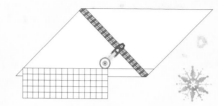

5. Each strip has a diagonal end. To join, place strips perpendicular to each other, right sides together, matching diagonal cut edges and allowing tips of angles to extend approximately ¼" beyond edges. Sew ¼"-wide seams. Continue stitching ends together to make the desired length. Press seams open.

6. Cut strips into recommended lengths according to quilt directions.

Mitered Borders

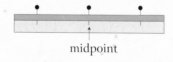

midpoint

1. Cut the border strips or strip sets as indicated for quilt.

2. Measure each side of the quilt and mark center with a pin. Fold each border unit crosswise to find its midpoint and mark with a pin. Using the side measurements, measure out from the midpoint and place a pin to show where the edges of the quilt will be.

3. Align a border unit to quilt. Pin at midpoints and pin-marked ends first, then along entire side, easing to fit if necessary.

4. Sew border to quilt, stopping and starting ¼" from pinmarked end points. Repeat to sew all four border units to quilt.

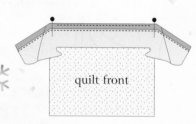

quilt front

5. Fold corner of quilt diagonally, right sides together, matching seams and borders. Place a long ruler along fold line extending across border. Draw a diagonal line across border from fold to edge of border. This is the stitching line. Starting at ¼" mark, stitch on drawn line. Check for squareness, then trim excess. Press seam open.

fold
stitch
back of quilt
¼"
trim

Layering the Quilt

1. Cut backing and batting 4" to 8" larger than quilt top.

2. Lay pressed backing on bottom (right side down), batting in middle, and pressed quilt top (right side up) on top. Make sure everything is centered and that backing and batting are flat. Backing and batting will extend beyond quilt top.

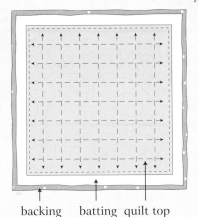

backing   batting   quilt top

3. Begin basting in center and work toward outside edges. Baste vertically and horizontally, forming a 3"–4" grid. Baste or pin completely around edge of quilt top. Quilt as desired. Remove basting.

Big Stitch Quilting Technique

If you plan to combine machine quilting and the Big Stitch Technique, complete machine quilting first. To make a Big Stitch, use embroidery needle with perle cotton, crochet thread, or embroidery floss. Anchor knot in the batting as in quilting. Make ¼"-long stitches on top of quilt and ⅛"-long stitches under quilt, so large stitches stand out.

Binding the Quilt

1. Trim batting and backing to ¼" beyond raw edge of quilt top. This will add fullness to binding.

2. Fold and press binding strips in half lengthwise with wrong sides together.

3. Lay binding strips on top and bottom edges of quilt top with raw edges of binding and quilt top aligned. Sew through all layers, ¼" from quilt edge. Press binding away from quilt top. Trim excess length of binding.

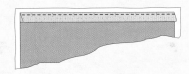

4. Sew remaining two binding strips to quilt sides through all layers including binding just added. Press and trim excess length.

5. Folding top and bottom first, fold binding around to back then repeat with sides. Press and pin in position. Hand stitch binding in place.

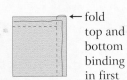

← fold top and bottom binding in first

Finishing Pillows

1. Layer batting between pillow top and lining. Baste. Hand or machine quilt as desired, unless otherwise indicated. Trim batting and lining even with raw edge of pillow top.

2. Narrow hem one long edge of each backing piece by folding under ¼" to wrong side. Press. Fold under ¼" again to wrong side. Press. Stitch along folded edge.

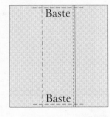

Baste

Baste

3. With right sides up, lay one backing piece over second piece so hemmed edges overlap, making single backing panel the same measurement as the pillow top. Baste backing pieces together at top and bottom where they overlap.

4. With right sides together, position and pin pillow top to backing. Using ¼"-wide seam, sew around edges, trim corners, turn right side out, and press.

Pillow Forms

Cut two Pillow Form fabrics to finished size of pillow plus ½". Place right sides together, aligning raw edges. Using ¼"-wide seam, sew around all edges, leaving 4" opening for turning. Trim corners and turn right side out. Stuff to desired fullness with polyester fiberfill and hand-stitch opening closed.

Discover More from Debbie Mumm®

Here's a sampling of the many quilting and home décor books by Debbie Mumm®. These books are available at your local quilt shop, by calling (888) 819-2923, or by shopping online at www.debbiemumm.com.

**Debbie Mumm's®
Quilts from a
Gardener's Journal**
112-page, wire bound

**Quilting Through
the Year with
Debbie Mumm®**
80-page, soft cover

**Debbie Mumm's®
Floral Inspirations**
80-page, soft cover

**Debbie Mumm®
Celebrates The
Holidays at Home**
80-page, soft cover

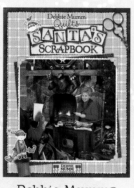

**Debbie Mumm®
Quilts Santa's
Scrapbook**
112-page, soft cover

**Debbie Mumm's®
12 Days of Christmas**
140-page, soft cover

**Debbie Mumm®
Salutes America the
Beautiful**
32-page, soft cover

**Debbie Mumm's®
Sweet Baby Dreams**
24-page, soft cover

**Friendship Quilt
Collection**
36-page, soft cover

*Book titles limited to stock on hand.
Products may be discontinued at any time by Debbie Mumm, Inc.*

Debbie Mumm, Inc.
1116 E. Westview Court,
Spokane, WA 99218

Toll Free (888) 819-2923
(509) 466-3572
Fax (509) 466-6919

www.debbiemumm.com

Credits
Designs by Debbie Mumm®

Special thanks to my creative teams:

Editorial & Project Design
*Carolyn Ogden: Managing Editor
Georgie Gerl: Quilt and Craft Designer
Carolyn Lowe: Quilt and Craft Designer
Jane Townswick: Writer
Laura M. Reinstatler: Technical Editor
Maggie Bullock: Copy Editor
Jackie Saling: Craft Designer
Kris Clifford: Paper Craft Designer
Nancy Kirkland: Seamstress/Quilter
Wanda Jeffries: Machine Quilter
Pam Clarke: Machine Quilter
Sandy Schreven: Seamstress
Bonnie Swannack: Seamstress
Tiffany Gerl: Crafter*

Book Design & Production
*Mya Brooks: Production Director
Tom Harlow: Graphics Manager
Heather Hughes: Graphic Designer
Nancy Hanlon: Graphic Designer
Robert H. Fitzner: Graphic Designer*

Photography
*Peter Hassel Photography
Debbie Mumm® Graphics Studio*

Art Team
*Lou McKee: Senior Artist/Designer
Kathy Arbuckle: Artist/Designer
Sandy Ayars: Artist
Heather Butler: Artist
Kathy Eisenbarth: Artist
Gil-Jin Foster: Artist*

Special thanks to Carolyn and Ted Lowe for allowing us to use their cabin for on-location photography.

©2003 Debbie Mumm
Printed in Hong Kong